The Cultural Devastation of American Women

The Strange and Frightening Decline of the American Female
(and her dreadful timing)

by
NANCY LEVANT

PublishAmerica
Baltimore

First printing

At the specific preference of the author, PublishAmerica allowed this work to remain exactly as the author intended, verbatim, without editorial input.

ISBN: 1-4241-3390-4
PUBLISHED BY PUBLISHAMERICA, LLLP
www.publishamerica.com
Baltimore

Printed in the United States of America

Dedication

This book is dedicated to my beloved mother and father, daughters, and granddaughters.

Acknowledgments

I wake up every day and thank God I was born an American woman in the 20th century. Thank God I am one of the few women in human history allowed to be heard.

Table of Contents

The Cultural Devastation of American Women

Preparing Oneself for Truth

I was born in 1954 and raised by an intelligent, stay-at-home mother and a gentle, self-made father. Today I am considering human history and its denial of 50% of the world's brainpower through the disregard of the female gender. And I realize that my birth year, my parents, and my place in history made me one of the luckiest women in all time. That's about as lucky as a person can get.

So I sit here today a woman in my 50's. I can vote, own property, marry or not, procreate or not, run a business, and make about 90% of all decisions that effect my daily life. Thank you, God, thank you for allowing me to be free from historic gender bondage.

There isn't a day that I don't think of women who continue to suffer enslavements of every kind and measure. And I realize that American women forget that many continue to suffer the indignities of gender control. We must always remember that most females, alive today, are not free women. We should be humbled by this fact. I want to help them. I want to do something, but first there's a problem – one that needs fixing, and so I, with my freedoms and my voice, write this book to my free, American sisters.

It is written with humility and love because I am an ordinary and imperfect person. I am not someone who would be heard on any large scale. No one would pay to see me in any arena. I am the lady who occupies the house around the corner from yours. I am the quiet, law-abiding person planting geraniums and impatiens in May and shopping at the super market on Saturday afternoons. I am the one caring for my grandchildren on the weekends.

I am not gorgeous, skinny, young, or especially talented. But I am a lucky and free and grateful American woman, and I want to talk to my sisters-in-luck.

Being both a reactive and methodical person, this book began in my mind in 2001 – the year our blindfolds came off and the year of my mother's passing. And after four years pondering, I realized that we, as American women, have lost many of our biological advantages over the last many decades. Many thoughts brought me to this conclusion beginning with my mother, who was "a lady."

She was raised by Christians. She wore dresses, painted her nails, wore make-up, and had her hair done every week. She did not swear. She was not coarse. She believed that "appearances" were important, and she believed that mannerly behaviors were a must. She believed in charity and kindness, and she believed mostly in her husband and children. She remained lovingly loyal to them until the day she died. My mother was born in 1912, and, bless her heart, she had imperfections, too.

Being born in 1954, I was actually two generations removed from my parents. I grew up in the 60's and 70's. I wore jeans and flowing dresses, dangly earrings, went barefoot, wore no make-up or bras, used the f-word casually, thought "appearances" were repulsive, and I believed that truth and liberalism were far more important than manners, family traditions, and cultural history.

I'm happy to say that her ways rubbed off in my adult years, but equally did my generation and my experiences as an American girl and woman – and I am grateful for them, every single one. However, I am also the person who, come hell or high water, was going to learn through experience. I never listened to anyone.

I will spare you, my neighbors, the details of my long history. It's pretty American-standard anyway – education, jobs, marriages, divorces, babies, kids' sports, house and home, birth and death—it's a lot like your lives with different names and faces.

But one path taken over 13 years ago did open a window of learning through pure and unadulterated observation. Thirteen years ago, I started an in-home daycare for children. It did not make me wealthy, but it allowed me to be a stay-at-home mom for my last child. It has been a good business, lots of write-offs, but my daycare did far more than I ever imagined possible. It provided a direct look into American families. From the most affluent to the poorest, struggling single parents, I've had the remarkable opportunity to observe, listen to, and witness families in their daily struggles to work, raise children, get by, and evolve in American culture.

And it saddens me to say that what I've seen, heard, and discovered is not so good. It's not good at all. Hence, and after several years of putting my impulsive thoughts into perspective and order, I've finally put my daycare experiences on paper. I am not an expert on human behaviors. I am not a genius in any way, but I am a free and educated American woman who is, in history, allowed to have voiced opinions. I offer them to anyone or no one, but hope someone will hear me, for I am worried about our country, and I am tremendously concerned about the women and children in the land of the free.

This book is not going to make women feel very comfortable. It may infuriate and insult many, many women. However, it is not the intention of this book or myself to insult anyone. I realized, in writing, that a lot of people were going to be antagonized by my views. I could hear people, in my imagination, saying, "Who are you to tell me what is wrong with me? Where's your Ph.D in my life? You're the baby-sitter – the hired help. You don't have the right to judge my life! And who made you the expert of anything?" I understand the attitude. I don't like anyone criticizing my life, my methods, or my choices. After all, I am a free woman and I can say and do as I please. But because of just that, I offer the following defense for my audacity: Experience still breeds knowledge.

I want an experienced doctor, lawyer, and chief. I want an experienced childcare provider, teacher, professor, CPA, and stockbroker. I want an experienced mechanic, furnace repairman, and veterinarian. You want, and deserve, someone who has the experience to give you credible thoughts and words.

Well, I have almost 13 years experience as a childcare provider, two children and three grandchildren. I have been a teacher, a social worker, and a family therapist. I've never been sued and no one ever called the police due to my improper care of children. So I guess the daycare chapters and references are based on some credible experiences. But, what about the rest of the book? Who am I to be talking about intuition, culture, God, women and men, to anyone? What credentials do I have that would dictate I should be listened to by anyone, ever? I'll tell you.

I have earned every credential and Ph.D that living gives. I am the person who could be despised because of this book. I'm the person who has made every single mistake that there is to make in marriages, child-rearing, employment, education, attitude, gratitude, sinfulness, bull-shitting, contemptuousness, shallowness, absolute self-absorption, vanity, and pathological judgments.

I am the worst of the worst. But I never, ever gave up on myself and my failings. I have come across one million acres falling, falling, falling, but always finding my footing – ever time. And that is the reason you should hear me – because I am still here, still trying, and because the only differences between your lives and mine are names and faces. We are supposed to fall in this wonderful and terrible place – over and over again. And we are supposed to get up and keep going until we know who we are and why we matter. I am not the person I was 10 years ago, 30 years ago, or 40 years ago, and yet I am that exact person and God's perfect creation.

I am qualified to speak by my life and my efforts. I am qualified because I am the ancestor to many who will come to suffer and shine in the world because of me.

I am nobody special. I am the lady in the house around the corner from your house. I have good days and bad days. I have a bad hip and a tongue like a steel trap. I plant flowers. I love my pets and I feed birds. I watch the news and fear for my children and grandchildren, and I continue a life-long dream of having a little house on Lake Michigan. I brush my teeth and I wash my face. I press my flesh to my jawbone and pull up, and I can still see in the mirror my beautiful, young self. I hold to all handrails now, and I detest the snaps of my knees. I am not fearless like I used to be. But I am clever and funny and ready to lunch with any good company. I have been loved and loathed, and I am sorrow-filled and dark and selfish, still. I have cared for and about your children. These are my credentials and my truth. I am you…so hear me.

Part I – The Children

Today's Moms

"A woman's work is never done." What a silly, sexist comment. We are all here to work and to pass life's tests and to get it right. All of our work, as people, is never done, and so consequently, we are always busy. But there are several issues concerning "women's work" that are troublesome. As a childcare provider, and in observation of and conversation with nearly 1,000 women, men, and children, five days a week, for many years, I can report the following givens for most moms of all ages:

1) Women are too tired.
2) Women are not cooking.
3) Women are bizarrely self-absorbed.

So, with many more lists to come in this book, let's honestly examine womanhood in 21st Century America. Let's ask how we are doing as females, mothers, and wives, and let's own up to a few facts about our cultural developments, and that we have changed enormously, and oftentimes, I'm afraid, not for the better. Let's examine how we operate, day to day, as free women in America. And let's look at our roles as mothers to American children. Let us also examine our roles as wives and career women, and equally consider the cultural pressures that have evolved into big businesses that now target our money and our gender.

We have come a long way from historic servitude and in a very short period of time. The cultural and educational changes to our gender are without precedent in human history. Much of what we encountered at the end of the 20th and now 21st Centuries are firsts for American women. We are pioneers in personal freedom, choices, education, and in the new American family that has evolved from our freedom.

Our responsibility to liberation and future women is enormous. Within a half century, the entire experience of female life has totally and completely changed. We need to think about this. We need to understand the scope and ramifications that the release from bondage actually entails, for it is a profound change in human history. And today, we find ourselves in a position of significant and global responsibility. We have to do right by our freedoms. We can never take them for granted or be stupid with freedom's development. So I believe it is important to track our progress and critically evaluate how we are coming along as liberated people. We are terribly new at almost everything that we now do, and we must be willing to act with care, caution, and to check our progress from time to time. We've had 50 or 60 years to truly grow into our freedoms. It's way past time to take a look at how we're faring.

I have not written this book as a labor of love. It is a book built on thoughts that have haunted me for some time. I am concerned about American women and their children. I see trends of behavior that do not make sense evolving alongside true human liberties. This book is a call to critical self-examination. It is written to demonstrate what I believe are obvious, dangerous, and obnoxious paths being pursued by today's Westernized women.

With this said, the book will insist upon self-evaluations that are going to be difficult as new cultural pressures upon free women are powerful and demanding forces. We have to honestly examine how we are handling the power to make daily and hourly decisions about everything that we do and say. So, let's simply begin with how we wake up and feel in the mornings.

I sense that women are stirred up upon waking. In fact, I believe many women awaken from night's sleep feeling tired, intense, annoyed, and an inch from anger.

There's tired and then there's tired. I'm talking about women who never, ever get enough sleep. But the peculiar observation is that exhausted women are staying up into the wee hours by choice.

- "I get my house work done late at night…"
- "It's the only time I can relax and be by myself…"
- "It's the only time I can think without being interrupted."
- "It's the only time I can be myself."
- "It's the only time I can get my homework done…"
- "It's the only time I can get through the mail."
- "It's the only time I ever have to myself…"

But instead of being physically tired from works, women are mentally aggravated, keyed up, and on edge. The truth is that they don't go to the bedroom until 1:00 – 3:00 a.m., and the late-night stay-up is actually an attempt to defuse themselves from what, I suspect, are pointless and unfulfilling events of their days.

When you see a tired child, tired from a day of activity, thoughts and stimulations of all sorts, you see a yawning, reclining, eye rubbing person who is nearly incapable of staying awake. However, I've heard 100 times from women who "get a second wind" at 10:00 p.m. and are ready to clean house or simply stay awake for four hours, knowing they have to get up at 6:00 a.m. to get kids off to school or to go to jobs. And from what I've heard, it's not men who are staying up all hours – it's the women, and it shows on their faces. You can always tell a tired women – she looks angry and overly made up, is always in a hurry, does not smile easily, and tends to be breathy without cause. Food for thought—for certainly, we've all seen this woman at least five times just today. Sometimes, she's me.

And speaking of food, meals are fast leaving the consciousness of the American female. This is of particular concern to me because for every group of children I've cared for in the past 13 years, half (yes, ½) of those children are too hungry and underfed or overfed with drive-thru food. I've seen hundreds of children who have never eaten vegetables and hundreds more who eat pizza, Taco Bell, McDonalds, and mac and cheese each and every night for dinner – each and every night. And I have seen at least 50 babies, under the age of one, who eat French fries, pizza, and burgers for dinner.

I've had one and two-year-olds arrive at seven o'clock in the morning holding zip-lock baggies full of chips, Cheetos, M&M's, sugar pencils, Skittles, potato sticks, cream pies, brownies, and Reese's Pieces. I've had at least 200 children come in the morning with fries from the previous night's dinner and sweet rolls and mini donuts from gas station mini marts. I've had two and three-year-olds arrive with Coke, Mountain Dew, and root beer in baby bottles and sippy cups. I've had hundreds of children arrive with fast-food breakfasts.

When I question parents, rich or poor, about what their children like for lunches, the standard, pat answer is "chicken nuggets and fries." I've seen 100-pound four-year-olds and 25-pound four-year-olds. I've seen at least 20 children who gag on food, no matter what food. And I've seen children beg for food the minute their parent(s) leaves my house. So, many years ago, I began asking all children who were old enough to respond, "What did you have for dinner last night?" And the answers, 90% of the times were, "pizza, Taco Bell, McDonalds, or macaroni and cheese.

One might be snobbish and think that only the uneducated would nourish children this way, but that snobbishness would be lost in fact. For it is an American fact most Americans feed their children way too much junk food, though they deny doing so. Just when you think denial could run no deeper…

I've had a mother relay that her five-year-old son ate more in my home in one day than he ate in her home in one week. I've had parents of four, five, & six-month-old infants, whose babies cry all night long in hunger, demand that I not feed their babies any baby food or cereal because their babies might then only take formula with food. Hello? I've had babies and toddlers vomit apple juice and milk because they only drink carbonated liquids.

I've had a two-year-old child of a multi-millionaire come to daycare every day with a satchel full of at least eight bags full of different candies, chips, and snacks, and I was instructed to let her eat them when she liked during the day. Of course, the child ate all eight bags of treats, and was lethargic at the end of the day. Her mother thought her lethargy was due to playing when, in fact, the child never, ever, moved off the couch because she was physiologically ill with sugar peaks and valleys.

Now the best-case scenario for morning nutrition has become cold cereal. If a child comes to daycare having had cold cereal, I thank God for that these days. Eggs, sausage or bacon, toast, oatmeal, juice and milk or fruit for breakfast? Not a chance…not any more.

Soup and sandwiches or fruits and salads—milk for lunches? No. Moms aren't around for lunches. Kids are in school, daycare, or mom's working, spa-ing, or in school. We already know about public school lunches. And mom's probably on Atkins or rabbit food only, and they would never subject their children to those diets – so, kids have grown up on fast food and worse, faster food. And me? I've continued to cook meals and dinners for children in my daycare. It's what has set me apart. Ham, green beans, and potatoes, eggs and sausages, meatloaf, broccoli and cheese, homemade soups—but often children don't like my food. Most have never had home cooked foods and they don't like them. I live in the house of leftovers.

Okay, so women don't cook anymore. They really don't know how to cook, as my mother's generation was the last to prepare meals as a rule. Thank God, again, that I had an older mother who taught me to cook and that I enjoy the time in my kitchen preparing meats and vegetables, fruits and, yes, even baking. So many women don't realize what they are missing. They don't know about the womanly arts, how it feels to give good, nutritious food to children, as many women now rebel against the notion of mom as family cook. Perhaps they feel such arts are enslavements, and yet most admire and respect Martha Stewart, one of my heroes. But, cooking also takes time and unselfishness, which leads me to another subject – beauty and self-absorption.

I have pierced ears. My 30-year-old daughter has a pierced belly button. Several of my young mothers have pierced noses, and, for the record, my beautician has a pierced eyebrow. And all of our mothers have complained about our piercings. It's a harmless pattern of natural beauty rebellion that runs through the eons between mothers and daughters. It's a good and harmless familial pattern that divides us a little and connects us a lot down the line. We females like to call it culturally defined "beauty."

"Beauty" is fun for females though beauty mysteriously remains in the eyes of beholders. Make-up, jewelry, pretty clothes in pretty colors…yep, it's fun. It really is. It's joyful fun when you're 10, and maybe a tad less so when you're 30, but honestly, I still get a kick out of a make-up day – even at 52. But let's be clear about one thing: I apply my make-up to myself and it takes five minutes. I wasn't born and raised in Hollywood and I'm not a television personality. I'm not a movie star. I'm not a model. I'm not a celebrity of any kind. I'm just one of many ordinary women who live in Small Town, Ohio, which, by the way, is a very small mid-western burg where many ladies my age wear glasses, jeans, decorative grandma sweatshirts, and have short, foofy haircuts. Well, at least we used to. Beauty, it seems, has taken on a life of its own and has even filtered into the small, mid-western villages.

I get my hair done once a year. I get it cut and sometimes colored. It's a $100.00 a year splurge that I allow myself…sometimes…when and if I have time. Truthfully however, I haven't had the time in five years so my hair is long and gray. But I've become the exception rather than the rule. To many, many women, beauty has become a very expensive, weekly, and time-consuming task. Let's look.

- Hair—$50.00 a week
- Nails- $100.00 up front, $40.00 per month upkeep
- Tans- $100.00 up front, $12.00 per week
- Make-up- $40.00 to $100.00 per session
- Botox- $250.00 and up

- Liposuction-$2,500.00 and up
- Implants and lifts—big bucks (the price of a car)
- Bleached teeth- $500 to $1,000.00
- Veneers- $2,500.00—$6,000.00
- Personal Trainers- $200.00 an hour
- Gym memberships- $60 to 200.00 per month

On and on—hours spent, family money spent—literally fortunes each and every year. And all totaled, about $6,000 a year—$6,000 a year taken from everyone in the family for the woman's sense of self-adoration. Then add the tips to all the beauty professionals and we'll make that a minimal $7,000.00 per year, and that's just for the basic beauty regimens. Add the big fixer-upper, implant, lipo, and re-plumbing jobs and the expenses are limitless.

How, you may ask, does that equate with my daycare business? Actually, in many, many ways—first and foremost, the message to female children is, frankly, repulsive. Secondly, the message to our male children about females is significantly repulsive and, thirdly, the fact that average, middle-class women have bought into Hollywood-style looks and grooming is shallow, dangerous, financially irresponsible, and makes American women look like shallow twits to the rest of the hungry world. In a nutshell, we have become so engaged in the act of self-adoration that we are losing respect from the youngest members of our society, our children, to the oldest members of the entire world.

Yet, these gorgeous, magazine-cover moms complain (and, boy, do they complain) about the cost of childcare—the fee for the care and feeding of their children – the ones they don't feed.

Think, for a moment, what the world sees on television about "us". Messages like, slice yourself up and look prettier, spend fortunes and look like models, do no labor lest you destroy your false fingernails, turn your skin into tanning bed copper tones, make your teeth shine like bug lights in the dark, and starve yourselves with meat or lettuce, or just starve period. Be 50 but pretend to be 20.

And then add to all the above the following: pay someone, anyone, to clean your house, care for your children, create and plant your landscapes, wash your cars, paint your walls, fix your leaking faucets, choose your "window treatments (they used to be called curtains and drapes)," decorate your children's rooms, buy your knick-knack and wall treatments (used to be called paintings), make your travel arrangements, cut your grass, kill your bugs, select your coordinated furniture groups, cater your parties planned by professional party planners, AND clean your pool. Shall I keep going? Do you know how easy it is to keep going?

My question is – what is going on? Why are middle-class families, who struggle financially like the middle class always have, taking a tenth or even fourth of their annual incomes for the sake of outrageous vanity and mimicking the wealthiest people on the planet? Where are your senses?

So, after I've had a child for 10 to 12 hours, a mother calls and asks if she may stop on the way home from work to get her nails done, or her make-up reapplied, or a comb-out, or to tan, or to stop by the gym for an hour. Now there's a message for the tired and hungry child who has been away from home for 10 hours! But mom will eventually come with drive-thru bags in tow. Women have placed their looks and appearances above the time they spend with their children and far above their children's health, and that's very peculiar when they are pathologically obsessed with their personal health and weights.

The abject self-involvement is to the detriment of their families, however women don't seem to care as they feel deserving of luxuries. All I can say is, you are wrong. The selfishness is pathological. The message is long lasting and dangerous to generations. Your grandchildren, of both genders, will feel the affects of your insecurities, self-loathing, your wasting of hard, earned money, and your selfishness.

Young and old, rich and poor, many mothers in American have changed. It is brutally evident in the McMansion communities where large, cheaply built houses are overly decorated, overly landscaped and planted, and overly sterilized by angry, strangely groomed women and their hired help. If you only knew the stories your children tell…

The Unhappy Family

When I was a child, every night the entire family used to sit around the kitchen table and eat dinner together. Imagine that. But even more remarkable, we used to laugh so hard at the table that we had to reheat our dinners in the oven…not the microwave, mind you…the oven – meaning 30 minutes later.

And after dinner, we did yard chores as a family. Leaves, weeds, trimming and pruning, sweeping, burning, planting, planting, planting, and never once did we ever, ever mulch.

Mulching…what a concept…ground-up trees, branches and yard waste marketed to control weed growth. Problem is, it doesn't. We all know that mulch doesn't control weeds. Concrete doesn't control weeds. The truth is that mulch, in its many, dyed colors and textures, adds one more layer of artificiality to our lives. It over-grooms yards just as we over-groom our children and ourselves. It smothers roots and subterranean life forms, and we mound it on year after year after year so that our yards look PERRRFECT. It is delivered, blown, or forked on by laborers, and is waiting for us when we get home with all the clean, sparkling edges of an SUV having just gone through its drive-thru wash. Look at those freshly mulched yards! Call the beautification committees!

The mulched and computer-landscaped yards of the McMansion neighborhoods have become so techno-sterilized and geometric that even balls in the grass, children, and pets look like scars on flesh. And this brings me again to thoughts of my daycare children, and how profoundly unhappy so many – more than half and nearing 75% of these children actually are. I thought you'd like to hear what I've heard from them – these little kids with the tanned and veneered mothers, houses, and yards.

One small digression: My daycare children certainly come dressed for the occasion. Diapered children in white, toddlers in $50.00 playsuits, and shoes that no mud or even grass should ever contact. They come with fur-trimmed hats, pacifiers, which are now called "binkies," their bags of junk food, and toys, which parents prefer other children don't touch. They bring baby laptops, tiny TVs, legos, and more pacifiers. In fact, today, I have 17 binkies in my drawer. That's a lot of pacifying. Seen and not heard is definitely back in child-rearing style.

And now, the other promised list of quotes from my very well dressed and pacified daycare children:

"I'm not allowed to go outside because of mosquitoes…"
"I'm not allowed to sit on a swing set because I might get hurt…."
"I'm not allowed to have anything with sugar in it…."
"I'm only allowed to watch PBS…."
"I'm not allowed to pet animals…."
"I'm not allowed to have pets because they're dirty."
"I'm not allowed to pick flowers…."
"I'm not allowed to talk when I eat dinner…."
"I'm not allowed to sit at the table…."
"I'm not allowed to sit on the furniture…"
"I don't have to eat vegetables…."
"I don't have to eat meat…."
"I don't have a bedtime…."
"I don't have to pick up my toys…."
"I don't have to say thank-you…."
"I don't have to do anything you say…."
"I don't have to be nice to the other kids…."
"I don't have to listen to you…."
"I don't have to read…."
"I don't have to eat…."

I could keep going but instead, I'll finish their last four words:
"…because Mommy says so."

American women appear to continue having predominant power in their homes and over children. This must surely be primordial biology rearing its head in 21st Century America. Children talk about their mothers to a far greater extent than their fathers, and children seem to learn communication skills from their mothers. They definitely learn the rules of behavior and eating habits from their mothers. Sadly, they also learn the beginnings of neuroses from their mothers' neuroses. Tiredness, hunger, intensity, sadness, irrationality, angers, sarcasms and bossiness, sullenness, mood swings, compulsions and obsessions – they so often come directly from maternal lines. And one more thing—an inherent disrespect by children for fathers also seems to come directly from moms. With that said, I offer more quotes from my daycare children:

"My dad is stupid."
"My dad doesn't like to be with us."
"My dad doesn't like it at home."
"My dad is a control freak."
"I'm not allowed to talk to Dad when he's working."
"I'm not allowed to talk to Dad when he's watching TV."
"Dad never does anything."
"I don't know my dad's first name."
"I don't know what my Dad does."
"Dad never talks to Mom."
"Dad likes his car better than us."
"Dad never takes us anywhere."
"Dad doesn't like to sit with Mom."
"Dad likes his computer more than Mom."

On and on...Do you think the three, four & five-year-olds come up with this on their own, or do you think they have heard this from someone?

So, I put my children's pieces together, and a picture of family life evolves. I see a man who is purposefully disengaged from his family. I see a woman who is tired, neurotic, and bored. She fills her days with beauty regimens, shopping, lunches with friends, or a job. She is built on the whole foundation of the history of women – mothers, wives, home-makers, cooks, maids, sex slaves, children whether or not wanted, laundresses, yard hands, seamstresses, and, she is above all, voiceless and powerless. In an instance of time, the "shes" in one section of North America are suddenly free. They go to work, first and foremost, to get the hell out of the house. And because most former "shes" have been discounted and mistreated, modern, American women feel entitled to everything, but there are no examples to follow. So they take the money they've earned and spend carelessly. They over-shop. And magazines and television showcase women in their new roles—beautiful, free, affluent, entitled, and under fed. But the most beautiful, free, affluent and entitled are "stars." And stars live like royalty with their make-up and hair stylists, clothing designers, architects and interior decorators, big cars, professional landscapers, and servants. And America's women find the examples they desire to mimic called perfection through wealth. And the more perfection needed, the less time for anything or any one else.

Husbands become hindrances, which turns them into annoying interruptions. Children become problematic because they take up too much time, get things dirty, need too much attention, and cost too much. So, for many years, women were faced with a decision: Is it going to be them or me? Exactly when the decision was made, I don't know, but for certain, women chose themselves over their histories and their families. And many say they deserve to come first. After all, a human history of gender servitude certainly entitles women to their time to shine and to grab some glory and attention. But what about the children who have lost their mothers to extreme self-involvement? Well, a few end results are certain. Children are hungry. Children are bored and sad though they have been given every toy and thing on the planet. Children are lethargic. Children are diagnosed with learning disabilities, depression, anxiety, hypertension, deficit disorders, eating disorders, and autism in droves and plagues in the United States. But, their mothers are magazine beautiful. Their yards are impeccable. Their houses are flawless and spotlessly clean. Do these perfections, perhaps, mask something that is imperfect – like the truth of lives behind mass-produced beveled glass doors?

Well, what do I know? I'm the help—one of the servants. But ladies, your children are unhappy – fundamentally unhappy every day. I hope this truth hurts at least as much as a Botox shot in the face, a boob job, or 35,000 pounds of mulch smothering the infant rabbits in your yard.

Lethargic Children and Learning

Some of my favorite kids are the ones who come to my home, stating they are only allowed to watch PBS, and then tell me their favorite cartoons are Ed, Edd and Eddy and Johnny Bravo. These kids are funny and sneaky. They've learned that their mothers are too busy to pay much attention to what they do. They are quick on their feet, clever, and play their mothers like 12-string guitars. They've learned that by being polite, saying they love mom, and being quiet, moms leave quickly, forget them instantaneously, and buzz off to their next selfish spree without worrying about what their children will do in the next 15 seconds. It's high theater for me, I'll admit. In fact, I can name a mother's true involvement with her child within a five-minute observation of the two. And I've also discovered that there are two kinds of uninvolved mothers: ones that directly admit their distancing from their children and ones that over-kill their involvement to the point of pure comedy. Either way, both rear lethargic children who are bored, ill fed, ignored, and soulfully unhappy. Several examples:

The mother-who-could-have-cared-less, who always stands out in my mind, was the mother of a three-year-old boy named Ben. Ben hated food. Ben weighed 20 pounds. Everything he ate, *everything,* made Ben gag, and so he learned to lodge all food in the right side of his face, between cheek and gum. Ben always had a giant cud in his mouth, which he sucked all day. I talked to his mother and asked for suggestions regarding his bovine behavior. She said, and I quote, "...give him French fries and potato chips...it's all he'll eat...I don't expect you to feed him because he doesn't like food."

"And what about liquids," I asked? "Oh, I forgot...I'll bring him something tomorrow because he won't drink anything you have."

"Even water," I inquired? "No, he hates water." And sure enough, the next morning, she brought Ben a two-liter bottle of Mountain Dew and a giant, tin jar of Charles Chips. I appreciated this mother. There was no pretense, no justifications, no nothing at all. She could have cared less for this child and was perfectly willing to share her disregard with me. I kept the child for two weeks and attempted to feed him, hydrate him, and I even called the grandparents to inform them of my efforts and concerns. They were a lovely, affluent senior couple who were also up-front and personal regarding their total lack of love for this child. So, I called Children's Services who, no surprises here, were also totally disinterested. I resigned as the boy's daycare provider and called the police the same day and never heard another word about 20 pound Ben and his honest as blue-blazes family. May God bless his life.

Another favorite parent was the professional, working mother of two children, who came to me with daily lists of expectations. And what lists they were!

1. No playing outside. They're allergic to the sun and dust.
2. No playing with pets. They're allergic to animals and fur.
3. No fruit. I prefer they only eat vegetables
4. No meat. They're vegan.
5. No television – ever.
6. No sharing of toys. I don't want them to get a virus from other children.
7. No candy, cookies, sweets of any kind or any wheat products, peanut products and, I reiterate, no fruits or fruit juices.
8. No holding hands.
9. No white bread.
10. No wheat bread.
11. No lying on the carpet.
12. Don't let them be in the same room with a child who is sick or who bites.
13. Make them nap two hours each day and at exactly the same time.
14. No milk, ever.

However, her oldest child ate chocolate cereal, with milk, every morning, taco bell or pizza every night, was six-years-old and weighted 30 pounds. Mom withheld food from both of her children, feeding the oldest pure garbage on a daily basis, and asking for a pure vegetable diet from me. I was also instructed to follow her orders to the letter of her laws. In her wacko universe, she wanted me to compensate for her maternal failings by inventing lists of compensations. However, she was so far out in left field that she stayed obsessively involved in the daily destruction of her sons' health and happiness. I tried to talk to her many, many times, but her issue was the need for control. She had no interest in her children whatsoever. She wanted to control them and me through me. And she also asked that I watch them late on Thursdays so that she could workout. And when she had all but starved and dehydrated her infant son, I confronted her. She was angry, but I tried to nourish those beautiful, little boys. What a world...

The best part of my day was when she left the boys and headed off to her office (a psychologist, no less). However, the diets of those little guys, and the over-mastering of them by their mother left them worn down and lethargic. The baby wanted to sleep all day from being awake with hunger all night, and the six-year-old was just tired—plain, old tired (depression), and would lie on the floor until his school bus arrived.

My tactics were to load him up with proteins, fruits and other carbohydrates. I gave him all the candy and cookies he wanted for the calories. He was getting stronger, gaining weight, and waking up from his fog and actually playing, but my greatest fear came to fruition when she realized her children were gaining weight and thriving and, sure enough, she pulled them out of daycare, which I knew that she would do. Why? I've seen this before. There are a lot of mothers out there who starve their children – a lot of them.

Poorly feed children not only can't learn, but won't. They don't feel good enough and their brains want to rest and shut off. How can I get this across to these smart, college-educated American women—the ones obsessed with their own diets, weights, and shapes, but seem to care less for the general health of their children. How can I attempt to cut through the denial? How about this?

Open your freezers and cabinets. What do you have stored for your children? And what happens to them when you turn off the television set in the middle of the day? Are they stressed? Anxious? Unhappy? Is the possibility of having to deal personally with you too stressful for them? Each and every day, when you ask them the same stupid question, "How was school?" and they simply have nothing to say to you, can you please, please take some responsibility and ask yourselves what has gone wrong in your homes? Are you even capable of hearing this, or are you simply angry with me for stating the truth? Are you inventing, in your minds, how to blame me or someone else, as I speak?

Your biology as women is fundamental to who you are and how you act toward children. If you find that you are not intuitive toward babies and children, and you really don't care as much as you think you should, and if you find that being a mother is stressful and boring you to tears, you absolutely hate to cook, you've arranged your lives so that you actually avoid all the primary functions of motherhood, and if you use or pay others to compensate for your refusal to act like a mother, then we are making progress because you are not alone. In fact, you are so very not alone that you are standing in a crowd of millions.

Together, my friends, let's keep our minds open and keep going and resist the urge to blame. Let's just look the beast right in the eyes and lay the cards on the table. And as everything I now say is turning into clichés, it's definitely time to move forward to the next issue: our houses – and this is a biggy, too, for all houses are a reflection of the people who live in them, and especially the woman of the house.

Hearth and Home

As far back as I can remember, I've wanted a house on Lake Michigan, with woods and a beach, and a big, screened-in porch overlooking that lake. In fact it has been a lifelong dream. In 1987, I actually renamed Lake Michigan to Lake Nanc, after myself. I used to say that Lake Michigan was the only thing I ever wanted to own. Now I look back and think– what an ugly thing to say!? I apologize to the lake and to myself. Sometimes it just takes years and years and years to stop thinking like a barbarian conqueror...

Home is an interesting and evolving place these days. True, it can still be your little dream house in the Great North Woods, but it can also be the condo by the mall, the apartment by the highway, the timeshare in Florida or the RV in the motor park or the trailer in the fishing camp. It can be the ugly McMansion that you wish a tornado would level or the historical Victorian that's falling apart downtown. It could be the $5,000,000.00 modern monstrosity on 100 acres hidden inside a conservation corridor, or a three bedroom one bath ranch near the strip mall or on your nearest Indian reservation. Home is a concept, for sure, but it is where hearts beat, rest, break, and lie.

Homes are the shelters we must have, as families, to survive. In other words, basic needs. I have a tendency to romanticize houses. I think it's because I loved my childhood home so much with its plaster walls and huge fireplace, its two parents, and fundamental warmth. I can recall every smell, the color of every room, the furniture, the wooden windows and doors, my parents kissing in the hallway by the banister—to me, my childhood home, which I occupied from ages three through 17, was safety incarnate, and I can't imagine my life's memories without it. But things in America have changed. Mothers and fathers don't stay with one company for their working lives anymore, and mothers aren't home to fill the houses with scents. In fact, mothers may be physically in the home less than any other member of the family these days.

When I grew up, women made the home. And women helped other women make their homes. They made curtains together, baked together, made children's costumes together, and they spring-cleaned together. Grandmothers always helped and were always making things for grandchildren. My grandmother made wardrobes of clothes for my stuffed animals and dolls, and grandmothers always made pies, cakes, cookies and special, old recipes for the holidays. Surely, all these memories should revolve inside the memories of children, but that's not what I hear from my daycare children. Once again, their commentary:

"My mom hates Christmas. She says it's only about spending money on stupid stuff."

"We went to Florida and we didn't get a tree."
"I didn't get anything I wanted."
"I got everything I wanted."
"My mom and dad had a fight."
"I only got a Play Station and 6 videos."
"I had to go to my dad's for Christmas."
"My mom had to go out of town."
"We went to a restaurant."
"We went to the mall to see Santa, but there were too many people so we left."
"Dad wouldn't go to church with us."
"My grandma wouldn't come because she hates mommy."
"Mommy says we're broke…"

I could go on and on. So the question is, what has happened to our cave in the world – our homestead, our warm and safe place? The first thing that comes to mind is that "living" in a house has become problematic for women because people get houses dirty and messy, and houses have become showplaces and art galleries versus homes.

It amazes me how perfectly clean houses have become and not by virtues of the women who live in them. I'm not talking about houses where sweepers are run and shelves are dusted from time to time, or even homes where dishes are cleaned up after meals. No, I'm talking about homes where each and every room looks like it's straight out of a decorating magazine. I'm talking about homes where children's bedrooms look like catalog pages and homes cleaned twice weekly by whole teams of maids. I'm talking about homes fully created by interior decorators.

Where do people function as people in these houses? The answers seem to be that they live with tyrant mothers who visit therapists if anything is out of place or out period. Gourmet kitchens that are rarely used, family rooms where food and drink is disallowed, shoes that are removed in decorator mudrooms, toys that are never, ever seen, and children who live in these homes without stimulation minus television or computer games and with mothers standing guard over the entire house like a security detail – and guarding what? Cleanliness? Perfection? Photo-quality rooms? And women wonder why children and husbands live in their bedrooms, behind closed doors, and find lives on the Internet.

And school and homework becomes the highlight of children's days because maybe, just maybe, their moms might relax enough to take a look at a math page. Actually, I've found that most moms pass that job on to dads and/or tutors, and prefer, if socially mandatory, to orchestrate "play dates" where, hopefully, someone else's house can be upset by children and their activities. Play dates, indeed...

And holiday decorations are delivered and set up by paid laborers and children wear velvet gowns and three-piece suits to celebrate holidays, and God forbid that they spill anything anywhere on the white carpets of the American home. And where pets are only tolerated as fashions bracelets for the lady of the house, as in tiny, toy, champion blood-lined dogs that children have to be so very careful around, but who escort mom to her informal social events.

These are the standard homes for millions and millions of American children, and again I say to mothers, your children are so unhappy. Think about it. You've created totally false and neurotic living environments where you expect children to thrive, yet you've given them nothing to interest them or stimulate their senses (an interior decorator can't do that), you've done nothing to give them joy (computers and giant televisions, and media rooms can't do that), or to make their homes desirable, comfortable, or safe in any way. No, homes have become manic decorating platforms for the chronically bored and insecure American female, and again, she has copied the lifestyle of the ultra-rich by turning cheaply built, overly priced houses into museums of social climbing and attention getting. Again I say, women, what has happened to your brains? What is this really all about? Let's keep going.

Child Care and Expectations of Perfection

Anyone in the childcare business knows that any mistakes, whatsoever, are a no-no. It is a business full of risks because children get hurt, fall, bite, hit, put everything including bugs and dirt into their mouths, get stung, and occupy the same dangerous world as adults. However, when you are paid to care for the children of others, there can be no accidents. Many a good childcare provider has ended service due to ordinary mishaps that befall children.

The expectations of parents are enormous and rightfully so. They pay good money to have their little ones properly cared for, and they want their children to be safe. But over the years, I've realized that my care of children must far, far exceed the care they receive in their homes. For instance, it is quite common for mothers to walk into my home at 7:00 a.m. and say, "Suzie wants bacon and eggs—scrambled, pancakes and apple juice – and she doesn't like butter but wants peanut butter on her toast." So, I take note realizing that I am not only the daycare provider but also the child's chef in the child's restaurant. Parents do assume that their wishes are granted and that I feed each child as directed and according to the child's daily wishes. Well, in these instances, one does the best one can. In this case, the eggs and peanut butter toast were fine, as was the apple juice, but there was no bacon on the menu for there was no bacon in the house. As for the pancakes, the eggs, toast and juice were plenty for the three-year-old. She did not need them. Then there are the other five children in the house to consider. But mothers are forthcoming about what children want—especially, I've discovered, when their children are constantly hungry to begin with.

When parents first begin a child in a daycare, the child typically arrives having been fed cold cereal, a bottle, or breast milk. However, after one or two days, children come to daycare unfed. My days always begin with cooking food and making bottles – always. This process continues from 7:00

through 8:30 a.m. until all children have arrived. You cater to the desires of the mothers and the children to ensure that nutrients are provided. Make note: Mothers escape meal number one.

Daycare lunches take place in two shifts: Bottle feeding first and then lunches for older children. Babies are marvelous in that they sense the need to sleep following their bottles so that mothers and daycare providers can tend to older children. Babies are very polite and considerate in this way. Lunches for older children are one of the most fascinating and telling experiences for childcare providers because they are a wide-open window into children's lives at home. For example, a five-year-old boy says to me, "I'll eat chicken nuggets but I won't eat anything green and I don't like fruit except for Fruit Roll-Ups." Okay, I say, and I heat up chicken nuggets, make green beans with cheese, and heat up leftover pasta. I place the lunch before the child with a glass of milk. He tells me he's not eating anything. I tell him that's fine, but that lunch is served and no other lunch but the one before him will appear. He eventually eats one chicken nugget, but nothing else, and the child is angry. After 45 minutes, I take his plate away. At 5:45 p.m., when his mother arrives, he bounds over to her the minute she opens the door and, quite literally, tells on me. "I told her I wouldn't eat anything green and she made me eat green beans and spaghetti stuff, and she made me drink milk." Mom very sweetly replies, "Okay honey, I'll talk to her..." Well, "her" is standing three feet away and the boy is clinging onto mom's leg, glaring at me. Mom quietly says, "Devon doesn't eat green vegetables and he really doesn't like milk or any kind of pasta. If you make him eat those things, he will be really stressed and he may get sick, so, for lunches, I'd prefer he had a Lunchable with juice or pizza or chicken nuggets and fries. Then he'll be happy and he won't give you a hard time. This mom, by the way, is also a schoolteacher. I smile, as if complying, and think to myself, "...Lady, if I had to buy Lunchables for daycare children five days a week for 13 years, I'd have to be a millionaire..." And, to myself, I continue, "...Well, this boy has her wrapped around his fingers and knows she will back him with the food issues..." So, I basically know I'm in trouble with this boy. It's either going to be his way, every day, or I will eventually be let go for not customizing my menu and my cooking to his daily orders. And I wonder—do mothers realize that I simply cannot comply with the daily junk food desires of their children without doubling or tripling my rates? And do they not want their children to eat well? In my opinion and after years of observation, I can tell you without question that it is the rare exception rather than the rule when mothers have any interest whatsoever in the diets of their children. What they care about is that their children get what they want so that they will be quiet and go away—appeasement to satisfy and silence. And I am definitely expected to follow rank. The norm is no longer health, manners, and nutrition. It just isn't. And make mental note number two: Mom escapes meal number two.

Another expected perfection has to do with children's clothing. When I grew up, girls worn dresses, and they all had to be ironed. I remember my mother ironing in the mornings in our kitchen every day. Play clothes, for me, were little one-piece suits, which also had to be ironed. My children wore little sweat pant outfits and other knitted play clothes—easy on, easy off, easy to wash, and no ironing. But today's mother seems to be a tad more formal. I believe many mothers still do laundry, but also hire maids who iron. Many, many children – particularly girls, but boys as well, wear awfully good clothing to daycare. For instance, khaki pants and shorts, Izod or Polo shirts, beautiful little cotton dress with matching pants, velvet coats, suede and leather (true!) jackets, leather shoes, and white…lots and lots of white clothing. Even baby attire has become extremely fashionable with specific styles, fabrics and colors.

Getting expensive clothing dirty is a major issue. I've had many, many, many mothers disallow the great outdoors due to the likelihood of dirt and stains. I've had many more ask for shoes to be removed before their children go outside so that the "shoes" aren't damaged. What about the feet? What about play clothes? Sadly, there are a whole lot of children out there with no play clothes.

I am also fascinated by the very typical clothing of four, five, & six-year-old girls – belly shirts, sparkling hip-hugger jeans with attached chains, platform sneakers, go-go boots, and bikini underwear. I'm fascinated when little girls come to daycare with their make-up boxes and their Brittany Spears CDs. Their mothers fascinate me, and how they came to points of brain death while still walking and holding jobs. Educated women, with college degrees, who have professional jobs (many in education), and who dress their little girls like redneck sluts and then provide sexual role models to boot. I ask myself, "Am I just an old fuddy-duddy, old fashioned, and being unfair and stupid? Have I turned into a critical, judgmental jerk? Have I lost touch with 2006 and what it means to be a female?" Maybe. Maybe not.

My take on the slutting up of little girls by mothers is this: What ever she wants she gets because I don't want to have to deal with her fits on any level whatsoever. Give her anything she wants, and I'm off the hook and we keep our communication at a minimum. Sound harsh? I don't think it is. I think today's mom would rather work than mother, would rather shop than mother, would rather groom herself than mother, and would rather talk to, be with, and participate with anyone else in the world but her children. Call me cold, but I don't think I'm wrong. It is a trend that continues to grow, year after year, and what is so frightening is that if the non-mothering trend becomes obvious, women may lose their children to bigger and more powerful entities. Don't think it can't happen. Don't think it hasn't happened ten million times in human history. Just today, you are forced to vaccinate, educate with the international 2006 curriculum of the government's choice; you have enforced proficiency exams, what is very, very close to mandatory national fingerprinting and DNA collections of children, and with one phone call from a neighbor who dislikes you, a child protection agency can come in and take your child away based on an accusation from a crazy who happens to live on your street. And never, ever forget that there have been many, many, many thousands of court-ordered and enforced sterilizations of women in the United States of America – American judges—who determined who was qualified to procreate. Don't think your fundamental rights as women and parents can't be taken. Don't think that de-population isn't on the global and "sustainable" burner.

Mothers better wake up and smell the cocoa. There are more children under the so-called protection of children's services groups in the United States than ever before, yet women are more educated and wealthier every single year. So why is life degenerating so horribly and widely for children in America? Why is their health deteriorating in epidemic proportions of obesity, diabetes, and eating disorders? And why are learning disabilities, behavioral disorders, and autism double epidemic?

Mothers, I only ask that we take a look at this and consider the possibilities. Changes are occurring with the most fundamental and biological relationship on the planet – that of mother and child, and though I sound like a broken record, your children are miserable though they have been given everything except, perhaps, you.

Clicks, Clacking, and Shunning

I'm a soccer mom. What a chore that is! You lose one soccer sock in the dryer and life goes to hell in five minutes. Soccer moms should be paid $250,000.00 a year and get three months paid vacation in the Bahamas each and every year for their soccer servitude. What an ordeal this sport has become, and especially when parents are seen as "the bad guys" by soccer organizations and coaches. Maybe one day we'll get that cleared up, too...

I've spent years sitting on soccer sidelines—heat, rain, snow, watching children and their families. And though you probably could have guessed, more opened windows and a few thousand more observations that continue my travels down the road of sorrowful opinion. Perhaps the reason why sport organizations and coaches have such disregard for parents is because parents are at least partially miserable people. Maybe more than partially...

I live in a fairly affluent area though I do not live in an affluent neighborhood. However, the bulk of my "local area" is affluent. So our soccer complexes are filled with fairly wealthy folks. They drive new and large SUV's, everyone has cell phones, and almost everyone is married. And as I sit on the sidelines, watching my darling daughter slam into an opponent in pig tails and braces, knocking her four feet forward as she collapses into a heap on the grass and cries for her mother, I notice that mother does not come. That would be a faux pas. Moms are not supposed to run onto the fields during games when their children are 10-years-old and injured...a definite no-no, upsetting referees and coaches and probably, in the long run, embarrassing our injured children (remember the part about "entities" having control over your children?), but my actual train of thought was focusing on the parents in their soccer chairs – their attire, their jewelry, their tans, their hair and make-up, their bright, white teeth, and their amazing and astounding attitudes during their children's youth sporting events.

The soccer moms are well dressed. Soccer is an expensive game to play, as, for example, is horse racing. In five years I'm expecting soccer moms will be wearing designer dresses and giant sun hats on the sidelines, but for now, they are wearing designer jeans, wind suits, and $100.00 sunglasses. They wear $100.00 sneakers, which coordinate nicely with the diamonds in their ears, on their fingers and dangling from their necks. And the tans and teeth! I can look down a row of ladies in October and see this color…this bronzy, pumpkin-brownish skin that highlights diamonds and high gloss white teeth remarkably. Those ladies do have white smiles. I guess time will determine how healthy those smiles will be in 20 years after being bleached and baked with ultra-violet light for two decades. But the soccer moms do look good and they certainly know how to groom. They all have the nice, short, sporty-bob haircuts, the same skin, teeth, clothing, and jewelry. And I think to myself, "This is all too Stepford for me," but then I remember, "…no…the Stepford Wives were really, really sweet and kind and were perfect, little workhorses." Today's soccer mom is none-of-the-above.

Anyone who has ever been involved with youth sports in the last decade or two, and maybe more, knows that American parents are beasts on sidelines. They are rude, cruel, cutting, unbelievably unkind, shaming, screaming, and downright mean. And the sparkling and remarkably similar soccer moms are, bar none, the worst of the bunch. I, myself, have even been guilty of being a barbarian from my soccer chair. May God forgive me. I understand that it's an easy excuse to blow hard, but I, in many ways, am far less refined than the cover-girl soccer moms. I don't have an image to defend, so it is creepy to see perfect women blow like sailors in up-scale suburbia at their children. I say to myself, "If they are like this in public, what must they be like at home?" And once again, I go to my daycare children, who are typically the younger siblings of their soccer-playing brothers and sisters. And, as I've said before, mothers – you wouldn't believe what they say:

"Mommy says my brother plays bad soccer."

"Mommy hates going to soccer with my sister."

"Mommy says my sister is the worst player on the team."

"Mommy says she'll never let my sister play soccer again unless she tries harder and scores."

"Mommy says my brother's coach is a [n] asshole."

"Mommy says Daddy is a big jerk at soccer."

"Mommy screamed at another kid and got into a fight with a dad."

"Mommy forgot to take snacks to my sister's game. She said, "…tough shit.."

Out of the mouths' of babes and into America's upscale suburbs. I wonder how many generations of children won't want to play soccer, a wonderful game? I wonder how many will be afraid to even try?

But another fascination at the soccer fields is the soccer mom clicks – those groups of socially leveled ladies, many of which living in the same subdivisions, who belong to the middle-class country clubs they can't afford, who belong to little social groups they create, who insist their daughters cheerlead in order to spread and grow their clicks—shutting out the majority of people and children in their towns. Those women who make bows for the soccer teams' ponytails and arrange social gatherings for the teams, who sit together at games and practices, and who shun, yes, I mean thoroughly and totally shun, all those who are not one of them. I am shunned. I am not married and that simply won't do, and I am far too direct and deliberate, but I know these women. They hate or at least disrespect their husbands. They are cruel to their children and fundamentally don't like them either. They want perfection. They seek social admiration. They want silent and sterilized children and homes. They are the queens of artificiality down to the absurdly large and unaffordable donations to schools to ensure that grades remain way, way above average. They are professional schemers and skilled at removing families from soccer teams whom they believe diminish their status. They don't like intruders and fear their own invisibility. They despise the ones who recognize their shallowness and they plan in groups to rid themselves of knowing parties. They are really something to watch. As they begin targeting their victims, they become nicer and nicer toward them. However, these women are mean and invisible as shrink-wrap.

And these women never, ever clean. They have impeccable houses and lawns that they never touch. In fact, the untouched home and yard is the perfect metaphor for the treatment of husbands and children – untouched.

Everything these women do sets them apart, literally, from people who are not like them, and it especially sets them apart from their children.

Children are messy, expensive, embarrassing, disappointing, hungry, time consuming, and they create mountains and mountains of laundry. They destroy bathrooms, bedrooms, and kitchens with dishes, crumbs, wet towels and muddy shoes, and they all leave sticky fingerprints everywhere. Magazine women cannot function happily or sanely in houses full of children. So, hence, careers or shopping, traveling, hired hands and servants, including childcare.

Now, mind you, and as I've said before, I am not an expert in the human condition or behavior or in any other subject. I am just an observer who has been given the opportunity to see through the eyes of children. If you find yourselves insulted, I'm sorry...but something is wrong with many American women and it is visible, obvious, and obnoxious.

Am I saying all women are like this? Of course not, but the pattern and the writing is on the wall when Hollywood extremes are now middle class norms. You can see and witness what I have said at any soccer game, in any town, in any state in our country, and these are America's middle-class moms. And though there are many, many of them, with their supposed money and social networks, I am telling you that they are riding on an edge of sanity. Perfection is too hard, they have constant financial problems, and they are far, far too devious and angry.

Entitlements

Living in America, and as American citizens, we are entitled to a lot. Our Bill of Rights and Constitution detail our entitlements. Some say they are dwindling. Some would be right. For instance, is the Patriot Act a good or bad thing when terrorists are the excuse for the elimination of our 4th Amendment rights – which happen to be gone? Should we be willing to give the Patriot Act time to attempt the capture "terrorists" who scheme to damage us, or are the terrorists our elected? Is losing any of our freedom simply too risky or necessary or legitimate? Food for American thought, but I do sense that "entitlements" have become more important than rights in our country.

Politically, I guess I'm either a conservative liberal or a liberal conservative. I don't seem to fit a political philosophy, but I wish I could, because I do believe that our government is a reflection of us and that we, too, are a reflection of our government. And, both we the people and our government have bizarre spending issues. Women are the primary spenders, buyers, and shoppers in America, and we buy mostly on credit. I would like to blame the government for this, because it does exactly the same thing – buys things it can't afford and does not have the cash to back up, and borrows itself into trouble. Same story. But even in our government's crazy bureaucracy, paper trailing, unfunded benefits programs, cover-ups, self-serving contractual deals with fundraisers, the Federal Reserve scam, on and on, women have different over-spending agendas.

Women know they spend incessantly on themselves – clothing, beauty regimens, jewelry, restaurants, shoes, purses, make-up, decorating, entertainment toys for children (big kid pacifiers), trinkets, and hired help. It's all about self-worship, self-loathing, and boredom. We can be frank, can't we?

Women have taken "entitlement" to another level altogether. When I think of the word entitlement, the following phrase comes to mind: "You are entitled to your day in court." I think entitlement actually means that you are qualified for a day in court or that you may go to court, because you are qualified to do so. You may be qualified by law, membership, or by insistence (jury duty), but the bottom line is that you "may" go to court. However, ask an American woman what she is entitled to in the land of the free, and step back while the list of the ages unfurls. Yes, there is an ethos of entitlement in America, and women feel entitled to any damned thing they want, and that is the bottom line. They have come to a place in history where they will be denied nothing. I pause as I write. I pause because this is difficult to think through. My intuition disagrees with my cultural up-bringing and my human history as a female. I pause, because it's not easy to make sense of it. As an American woman, I can educate myself in any profession I chose. I can marry or remain single. I can sleep with my husband or sleep with as many people as I want. I can have children inside or outside of wedlock (what a word). I can care for my children or hire someone to do the job for me. I can send my children to boarding schools and see them at Christmas and for summer vacations, or raise them in an alternative family, such as a commune or co-op. I can work, go on welfare, live in Mexico or Ireland. I can own a house or live in a science station in Antarctica. I can do whatever I want, whenever I want. I can leave my husband because he bores me. I can sign over custody of my children to my boring husband because I want to be free from all servitude. I can make tons of money, be an artist, be openly gay, live with a boyfriend, become a nun, a prostitute, or run for office, and I don't have to ask for anyone's permission, blessing, or advice. I can do what I want when I want. Sounds selfish, doesn't it – even childish—if the child was extremely shallow and stupid. But...another but...American men have had rights like these. Wealthy people have always had rights like these. It's not as if total, personal freedom is unique to women. There have been millions and millions of examples of spoiled and reckless freedoms taken by people throughout history. Self-importance and adoration breed self-entitlement, as does pure selfishness. But then, I say to myself, women are entitled to a lot. We do deserve a lot of freedom. But people, truth be told, entitlement is a far cry from freedom. In fact, I'm not sure that I even like the word entitlement. What are we entitled to? To spend families into bankruptcy? To lavish ourselves with trinkets? To feed children horribly and knowingly? To act critically and disdainfully toward those who are less affluent? To act immorally and call it freedom? To live off the government's money, which is the money taken from the daily labor of working people? To play and spend for a lazy living and call it truth?

If you get up in the morning and give your child sugar cereal out of a box, turn on the cartoons, and lounge around doing whatever suits your fancy for the next six hour, than what good are you to anyone or any cause under heaven? I'd call you purposeless. So why would you be entitled to absolutely every luxury you wanted? Why?

Here's what I think all people—men, women, and children are entitled to:

- To ask for help and to help others
- To work
- To help animals who are now squeezed everywhere on Earth because of humans.
- To realize that money belongs to everyone in the family.
- To God
- To children
- To basic kindness

No one is entitled to the following:

- A free ride
- Dictatorship, which means getting your way all the time
- Laziness
- Shallowness
- Financial conning
- Cruelty
- A belief that your life or lifestyle is above anyone else's – class conflict has always, always, always led to wars.
- Servants—You can always ask for or hire help, but if keep hired servants on a weekly basis, you need to think again. I don't care who you are. The message and the division between master and servant is too dark and great and has caused seething and undercurrents of hatred throughout history. In America, can we please stop with the servants!! There might be 10,000 people in the entire country who actually need staffs of people to help them on a daily basis, but no one needs servants in suburbia. NO ONE.

Sometimes my daycare children talk about their other "mommy's helpers." It is common that children are very, very fond of maids. And I wonder if anyone reading this book will pick up on the subtle kick in the teeth that the sentence prior to this one provides? I think I'll write it again: It is common that children are very fond of maids. Hummm. I not going to touch that with a ten-foot pole. Entitlements, indeed...

The Self-Rewarding Machine

Don't you get tired of the talking heads that want you to feel guilty for watching TV? Quite frankly, it's the only form of entertainment I can afford. The days of big league games and concerts and plays are over for me. In fact, they were over 25 years ago, because they were unaffordable then, as well. They have become the venues for the rich or the singles with no kids. They are too expensive for the middle-class, so we watch television. Then we are told by "experts" that we are wasting away due to TV. My response to them is....Go...away. I've been watching a soap opera for about 25 years. I love it still, and my mind is not rotten. My grandmother also watched a soap for decades. She called it her "program." Her mind was not moldy. And yes, our children watch a lot of television. Perhaps that's because there's a lot to see—wholesome and unwholesome, but a lot. Perhaps it has to do with a strangely, dangerous world, whereas, unlike myself as a child, children cannot go out to play and come home six hours later for dinner. Perhaps the television habits of our children (and us) are the result of the addiction marketing strategies of business and government. Perhaps children, with their parents, are doing exactly what entities want them to do as they pass time watching the box.

I do promise you that I will address and persecute garbage TV in this book, but for now, one of my favorite television shows is my local government access channel, where I can watch my city council meetings each month. I would like to challenge every reader of this book to watch their community's government access channel, and specifically, your televised city council meetings. It's time we all got involved in community politics, and the best way to begin is to watch, learn, and listen to how the powerful get and stay that way. I challenge you to watch three council meetings – one a month for three months. And what you will see is the pattern of self-rewarding.

You will see the Mayor present a plaque to the Chief of Police. You will see the City Manager present a plaque to the Mayor. You will see the Fire

Chief present a plaque to the City Manager. And you will see all of them present plaques to all the Committee Men and organization heads and officials. Each and every meeting, you will see a rewards system, with plaques in hand, naming each recipient a hero or a humanitarian or a human servant or a best in show in one manner or another. This system builds resumes and vitas. This system builds professional credentials and politicians. And it never stops. It is a powerful machine and it is subtle. And we, the public, are clueless.

This system filters down into the lesser entities like the community "clubs." They, too, self-reward whereby building agendas and paths to the top. This is all very clever, for who would not elect a humanitarian hero with a wall of plaques? All I can say is that our stupidity is counted on by our elected heroes. Ask yourselves what they have really done. You will find they've done nothing at all minus politic. Don't be fooled by this manipulation, which can be viewed in every city in the United States on your television. Watch your TV. The upper and upper-middle classes have always self-rewarded. It retains their power and position. Don't be fooled. There may be one hero out of a million, and chances are, that hero will be some average Joe or Jane who ran into a burning house to save a child or a dog. When was the last time your mayor did that?

This practice filters into youth sports, civic groups, and every other social arena where one finds the "climbers," or shall I say "partners." And it has certainly found its way into the strategies of women.

The self-rewarding missions of the middle class cause poverty, empty refrigerators, and extreme vulnerability. All the plaques and engraving by the upper classes are, after all, paid for by us, the taxpayers, via budgets. It doesn't come out of their pockets, but the nickel and diming that we inflict upon our families and ourselves hits us directly in our lifestyles and credibility.

The overly-decorated house, with walls covered with pretty, little stuff, 25 candles in the bathroom, dressers overflowing with jewelry, closets stuffed with clothes, and the knick-knacks – hundreds of pointless, useless "things" that we buy because they are inexpensive, and clutter our homes with senselessness—it's mindless self-rewarding entertainment, but gains no advantage for the family. Knick-knacks bankrupt families, and for what? Do your children worship and adore the crystal candlesticks that are never used? Do they even see the copperware and glass trinkets and plate collections on the walls and tables? Are they allowed to touch or use them? Why do we buy these things when we are cash poor in debt?

The difference between the upper and middle-class is that the former spends other people's money to create wealth for themselves. We spend our money to mimic them. This is stupid, and particularly so when you frequently run out of groceries to feed your families, and find yourselves waiting three days to buy milk or charging it on a credit card. And consider the message to children. They will grow to expect that their homes be adorned and that groceries can wait.

Let me offer more commentary from my daycare children and their parents to illustrate my points:

"Can I have some milk because we don't have any?"

"I love ham. We never have ham."

"We don't have dinner. We get it at a restaurant or my grandma's house."

"Do you have any shoes that fit me?"

"Can I have a cookie? Mom says we can't afford to get any."

"They haven't had any breakfast because I can't go to the store until Friday."

"Can you give Johnny $2.00 for lunch money because I'm broke. I'll pay you back Friday."

"I forgot my purse. Can you loan me $5.00 for gas, and I'll pay you back Friday?"

These questions are very, very common. I get them each and every month from two-parent families, both employed, and both broke one or more times a month. They ask me, the hired help, for loans, and they live in houses that are three times the size of mine and have automobiles that never, in my entire life, would I ever be able to afford. And they have weekly maid and lawn service, weekly hair and tanning appointments, gym memberships, and no food or savings. Go figure.

The habit of self-rewarding is political by very nature and destructive on every level. We were not meant to be vulnerable, senseless, and stupid. We were meant to be prudent, sensible, and providers for children. So my message is this: Watch your televisions. Try to avoid trash TV so that you don't corrupt your minds with political propaganda trash; know what your local officials are up to, and save your money. Don't trade New York for beads or airbrushed fingernails.

Religion, War, and Women

I was raised in a mostly agnostic family. However, I needed faith, hope, and love. I tell myself that my lack of religious training actually allowed my beliefs to develop naturally and without influence or indoctrination. In ways, I consider myself lucky to have survived American culture. However, that culture also allowed me religious freedom and atheism to many in my family. To this day, I struggle with how to worship freely and without indoctrination in the United States. Every Christian sub-group insists that their road to the pearly gates is absolute. Protestants and Catholics and Latter Day Saints are individually and absolutely positive that their religious stories and histories and rules are God's requirements for salvation. So many years ago, I started my personal investigations into the world's religions. I began with Christianity with a very Pentecostal bent, and I found fundamentalist rules to be rigid and peculiar. Then I studied Hinduism and discovered that a born and raised American cannot possibly fathom the nuances of Hinduism without life-long instruction, guidance, and India, and I simply knew I could not be Hindu. So I studied Buddhism and realized very quickly that I was not a Buddhist because my personal sense of God, I believed, required a personal and human purpose for my being on the planet. I needed to have purpose. So I studied the Koran and realized that, as an American women, I could not lose my freedoms to men. So I studied Judaism and felt pretty connected. But Judaism was split three ways in America: Orthodox, Conservative, and Reform, and each thought the other either radical, perfect, lying, or too liberal. One says the others are unfaithful, one says the others are extreme, – so, for me, Judaism was unsettled within itself and globally. How does one pick between the Judaism of Crown Heights, Israel, Zionism, or the Reformed? How was I supposed to figure it out? So, I went back to the basics of the Bible. I also studied the Book of Mormon at the request of a Mormon friend. The Book of Mormon is an interesting book. It provided some sense to Westerners and their roles as Christians more, perhaps, than does the Christianity of ancient Israel, its war with Judaism, and the whole "chosen ones" issue. But I have cultural and intellectual struggles with the Church of Jesus Christ of Latter Day Saints, as well, though I continue to study the scope and ramifications of their rituals, beliefs, and rules, which also seem rigid.

What I have discovered over the years is that believing in God is the easy part, but the acceptance of the human politicizing, and hence, bowing to the expectations of religious leadership, is dangerous. The current "global war" demonstrates this to perfection. I believe that the willingness to declare a belief in God carries great responsibility and great risk. When we, as Americans, declare we are Christians, we, too, are not settled in any way, shape, or form on what exactly that means. We've never been able to reconcile Christianity with science. We've never come to terms with being a predominantly Christian country with freedom. Let me explain. We are free to be gay. We are free to abort. We are free to fornicate. We are free to divorce. We are free to starve our children while belonging to country clubs and driving $45,000.00 automobiles. We are free to envy and want everything superstars are and have. We are free to attend or not to attend church. We are free to work on Saturdays and Sundays. We are free to kill in wars, and to steal via bureaucracies and loopholes, on and on...In other words, and with the kindest criticism I can think of, religion in America clashes with America. I don't know what it means to be religious in America. It depends on who you talk to and the agendas of millions of people and institutions. I do, however, know what it means for Nancy Levant to be a religious person.

To me, religion transcends people's politics, or is supposed to. Religion in America has been used to bully the constituency and to get votes. I can't reconcile political worldliness with faith. So I tend to quietly personalize my beliefs and feel mostly alone with them.

99% of all my daycare children have never attended church. Very few attend once in awhile. The tens of millions of children playing select sports don't attend churches because they have Saturday and Sunday games and tournaments. And yet, God exists for most people, and Christianity, as well as most other religions, states that the Sabbath is holy. It's all a huge quandary and it has become political on all fronts – even via the requirements of youth sport organizations that claim that competitive games trump the Sabbath.

So here I sit, a mother, a believer, and living in America – supposedly the most free country in the world. What is my role as a women, raising a select soccer-playing child, who believes in God, and who sees frightening flaws in her culture? What do I teach my child about God? Do I say it is unnecessary to believe publicly? Do I say that American culture and religion are at war, and yet she has religious freedom? Do I tell her about the political intent to dismantle the Christian religion, and to replace it with an environmentally-based religion manufactured by political think tanks? Do I say that it is necessary or unnecessary to attend churches, and if she attends, does a commitment (and Commandment) to the Sabbath override soccer? Do I say nothing and let her figure it out on her own, the way I did? Do I hand her over to a church and let others dictate faith-based and non-profit rules? I don't know. But I think this is more than food for thought for American women. Many more children are now raised without any faith whatsoever. Many believe this is a good thing because religions are famous for waging the bloodiest of angry and unwinable wars. Many think that you should be free to choose, but then, no matter which flavor you choose, the others say you've chosen badly, and that your soul is in jeopardy. Our government thinks they should choose for us. And then I wonder what a Holy Being thinks of the great disconnect between religious truth and religious doctrine. Obviously, we as people can't figure it out. We never have as a species. So, in my lack of knowing and my ignorance of God, I return to the help of my intuitions and instincts because I know I cannot make sense of the discrepancies between faith and the agendas of the religious and the political. I try to use my intuition to sense and feel my relationship with my beloved Holy Being. I pray for guidance and wisdom. I pray for help and clarity. Sometimes in prayer and reflection, God is present, felt, and known. Sometimes there is clarity and I know what I need to do. But I wonder if American women even remember that we are spiritual beings, connected to God, when we are so removed from our children and our biological gifts as women. And I wonder how we expect that our children and husbands will stay sane amidst this horrendous disconnect. Women have known throughout their entire human history that the giving of themselves has lifted the human condition. Why did we stop? For jobs? To work out? To go to the mall and drop our children off at the sitter's? To go the country club? To bleach?

A large part of the giant disconnection between people and God in America has a lot to do with women. Sorry, but facts are facts. When we hold the keys to the homestead, we simply have to consider that something is amiss in our families when American culture is foul with rampant corruptions of every kind and in every institution. We're raising the people who become corrupt, and we simply have to point our fingers toward home to figure out what has gone so very wrong. Tis true.

Woman as Muse

Art tells us that the primary muses throughout human history continue to be God, love, and war – the three greatest causes of suffering on the planet. Peachy.

God the Muse—what can one say? It seems that all religions and their sacred texts dictate the future for human beings. And yet, we have "choice." What does that mean? By virtue of the fact that God made the playing field so difficult, huge, and complex, we fight for God. We are even told the outcomes of our battles beforehand, and at the same time in scriptures are told "...but you have choice." Does that mean we can choose to stop fighting and save the species, or does it mean we pick a side and fight? Does it mean that all religions predict they will take over the world's people and their souls? What can one say when, and still, after thousands and thousands of years, we can't or won't figure out how to believe? God is the perfect Muse. We can never get it right. We can never figure it out. We operate on pre-existing outcomes, written thousands of years ago, fearing them, but we have choice. Gee whiz...the inspiration, like the universe, is endless. Religious war is endless.

A four-year-old asked me if saw "Samma bin Laden." I was speechless, not because I was asked, but because I didn't really know what to say. (For a paid childcare provider, it's one of those loaded questions that can get you into trouble. Questions like, "..do you think mommy should marry my dad?" or "..do you think my daddy is mean?" after mom walks in one morning with a black eye. These questions from children are very tricky.

"Yes," I tell the child. "I've seen him on television."

"Mommy says we're having war."

"Yes. Something like war."

"Samma's in the war..."

"Yes, I believe you are right."
"I saw smoke on tv."
"I've seen the smoke on tv, too."
"I don't like it."
"You know what? I don't like it either."

And when I was his age, there were wars on television, too. In fact, there has never been a time in my life when wars were not televised every day. War is endless television. And it has made us all nuts. More informed? Oh, yes. Smarter? Doubtful, but it has made us nuts – internationally. When four-year-old children are talking bin Laden and smoke, God help us all because these "wars" are just too much. Even if one or the others becomes the last wars for the human race, they are still domineering and in my face, and I don't like it. I don't want my children, grandchildren, or daycare children seeing, hearing, and feeling like I did, remembering clearly, and to this day, the Vietnam War Show. I hope the world's writers, sculptors, musicians, and painters are thinking about these wars. I worry that this "thing" is too grotesque and loathsome for artists. I'm not hearing about WWIII art. I'm not seeing it unless called Michael Moore who is a social/Socialist commentator, but not artist. If these wars are muses, they're not mine by choice.

No, in fact, this is an anti-muse war. I want the opposite of this war to be my muse. I want comfort and ease of mind to move me. I want the peace of a happy childhood, and I'll lay odds that I'm not alone. I think the world is longing for pastoral experiences and memories, and instead, we get bin Laden, smoking buildings, body parts, and televised political-religious war and its talking heads every single day and evening of our lives. And perhaps our fear is orchestrated fear to serve political intentions. Wouldn't be the first time, now would it?

And then there's love. The muse made of God's greatest virtue, the desires of the hearts of men and women. At its best, love is profound and incapable of definition. It is holy and of the spirit. At its worst, it is sadness incapable of definition and can turn into rage and hatreds in five seconds. It is the stuff of poetry and literature. It is our greatest obsession, need, and thorn in our sides. It is a perfect muse. But love requires romance—that people remain capable of its mysterious ways. And without both genders being capable of romantic love, no muse lives.

Women in literature have long been muses. Their beauty and mystery as females have stirred and propelled men throughout human history to acts of bravery and chivalry and have given men purpose. Love was to be fought for and won, defended, and protected. The love for women has inspired, moved, and civilized men. But their fascination with women has always been based on their ability and willingness to romanticize the female. The soft, the young and beautiful, the protecting and caring for the gentle natures of females are what have moved men to straighten up and fly better in the world of love and war. Woman as muse is fundamental to human mythology, history, and art in every culture. True love is valued in all cultures and is still the ideal perfected in the dreams and imaginations of genders. True love is based on God's love for his creations in all religions and why marriage between genders remains the model for all the world's peoples. Marriage between genders is supposed to be the final outcome of true love, which, in literature, is romantic love and children. In the modern era, and particularly in the Western world, times have changed.

Homosexual love has mainstreamed into Western culture. Marriage has become unnecessary for women and children as women have gained economic opportunity and power, and procreating outside of marriage has become a right of choice. Is this human progress? Many believe it is. I am not intelligent or spiritually advanced enough to judge people and their choices in this culture. I still jump from political manipulation to political manipulation at times, but again, I return to my daycare children. What I see and hear from them and their families is that changes in the roles of mothers and fathers and their relationships with each other have not caught up with fundamental and emotional needs of children. I see ungentle and un-nurturing mothers and what looks like bored and disconnected fathers. I see the tension between parents every day as one or both parents drop off or retrieve their children. Commentary that I hear from parents, like:

"She didn't bring his jacket?"
"Did he remember to pay you?"
"I'll do it because he will absolutely forget."
"I'll do it because you will absolutely forget."
"Did he pick up [child's name], and what time did he get there?"
"Have you heard from my wife? Did she call you?"
"I don't know anything...ask her..."

It's an undercurrent – a darkness that comes to the surface of the one-liners I hear every day, and it tells me that parents are disconnected, untrusting, blaming, and angry. And the undercurrent is the rule vs. the exception. There is a fundamental disrespect and lack of trust in competency between mothers and fathers, and the children know it. They see it, and they talk about it:

"Mommy says daddy is a idiot."
"Dad says mommy should cook dinner for us."
"Dad is never home."
"Daddy says mommy is never home."
"Mom doesn't like dad's work."
"Daddy says mommy works all the time."
"When's mom coming?"
"When's dad coming?"
"Who's going to pick me up?"
"Why are they always late?"
"Did mommy forget to get me?"
"If they don't come, can I stay with you?"

On and on and on. So what happened to the young couple that loved and married each other one, two, and/or five years ago? Romantic love ends with children in America? One wonders. Do the demands of the culture with its two-income, 12-hour a day job requirements, its expenses and adult entertainments all but lessen love and the happy family? I'd say, yes...could be. The demands and the costs are too high. The homes cannot be made because the adults living in them are too selfish, busy, and self-involved to realize that their desires as individuals clash with the needs of the family. In fact, I'm willing to say that, on a daily basis, I see mothers and fathers who can't stand each other. I see men and women who blame each other for the failure of family happiness. But what is more interesting is that I see women who really don't care because they have options, and they know it. They can leave the marriage and draw child support. They know the children can go back and forth between parents in divorce, and know they will have some free time from their children if they divorce. Sometimes you can see and hear the wheels turning as they consider their options, and sometimes you can see men waiting – waiting to see what she will do and what it will cost him. Sometimes you can see his anger rising, and you wonder how he will act if she leaves. And you see the stress in children while they wait for someone's shoe to drop—wondering what their futures hold.

American women aren't muses anymore. They're too busy and self-involved to be the poetry of men. And it's sad because I have the sense that young men, who fall desperately in love, are doomed by time and by knowing his love truthfully. What will he see a year after his marriage? Who will his beautiful bride become in America? Will he know his bride at all in two years? And will she care if he doesn't?

With a 50-60% divorce rate in the United States, tens of millions of children reared by multiple fathers and boyfriends, and men angered and wounded by each and every divorce, perhaps woman will become unwanted, too. Worst-case scenario? American men rid themselves of woman as muse and opt for religious war. American men begin a slow but deliberate march of disregard for women and slowly change their minds about females as a gender. Don't think it can't happen. Look at Iraq, Iran, and Afghanistan. Look at their women who, 35 years ago, were physicians, lawyers, politicians, and university professors. Look what happened to those women under the control of angry men who decided to set them back a few thousand years. Don't think it can't happen.

But as we know, true, muse-worthy attraction is very hard to maintain. Closeness breeds the full and complete knowing of the one yelling for more toilet paper, snoring, passing gas in the bed, and belching at the dinner table, and, at times, smelling as ripe as Roquefort cheese. But still, we need our fascinations with each other. We need to remember this because when genders get really angry, culturally angry, and frustrated over several generations, bad things can happen to women and children. Men need women. And yes, they need us more than we need them in today's world, but knowing so, they also need us to be their muses and their one true love, which is really a trusted, life-long confidant, lover, and friend. Don't mess with Mother Nature. She is, after all, one tough broad though very, very wise.

Husbands in a Hand Basket

As I look at and think of all the little boys whom I've had the honor of caring for, I imagine them in 20 years—married, working in careers, and raising children with their wives. I also think of the history of the male gender—its barbarism, disrespect, and cruelty to women and children. And as slow as molasses as men seem to evolve as human beings, American men have come leaps and bounds from the tribal thugs they have been for eons. Their changes have come, perhaps, with dragging feet, yet they have become less violent and more respectful of women and their opinions in many, many ways. In the great scheme of time, American men have done beautifully though perhaps it is due to the fact that they had power to begin with, and, for the most part, still do. The transition of women, from servants to freedom, has been a terribly rapid and challenging ordeal. One of the primary reasons for this challenge, I feel, is that women over the centuries knew they were intelligent and abused. They knew their brainpower was wasted and that they were mistreated. They knew they had wisdoms to offer to the world, but they were denied access to the world and its needs. And they were told their opinions were foolish, childish, and useless. Women always knew this was wrong. So for thousands and thousands and thousands of years, women had to stay silent. But their minds were working. It is my opinion that women have experienced the longest period of pondering in human history. They simply thought about all the things they could not do, or say, or feel, or have, or own, or contribute, or invent, or read, or try. And during these millennia of thinking, they raised their children, grew food, cooked and cleaned and sewed and created the fundamental base of civilization – the home. But their minds were evolving in silent thought while their babies came, one after another after another.

And finally, in the west, the Suffragettes conquered Western history. And what came after, and from then on, was rapid-firing and fascinating cultural changes. Women went from the home into the world. They changed the courses of elections, employment and benefits, marriage, and they changed American men's opinions regarding women as a gender. Moms became super-moms, handling careers, children, husbands, large homes and yards, and automobiles. Most American women handle the family money and pay the bills, and many American women earn higher wages than their husbands.

We are doctors, lawyers, senators and congresswomen, judges, religious leaders and soldiers. We are holding some of the most powerful positions in our country, and our country is better for the contribution of many women. America is now using the brainpower of both men and women, and it certainly hasn't hurt. But...

There is always a "but..."

The empowerment of women did come at a cost, for the rapid cultural change brought changes never before faced in human history. Altering the foundation, which is the family, is a damned big issue. Women leaving the home for employment and educations meant that mothers no longer primarily raised millions and millions of children. Children had strangers and union teachers to rely on for food, cleanliness, teachings, social skills, motor skills, companionship, and propaganda. Homes were no longer the domain of women but the charge of people hired to keep them. And as food evolved into boxed, canned, and fast food, employed women no longer needed cooking skills. As the one-income family evolved into the two-income family, more money meant larger homes, multiple cars, and more laborers. And as the eight-hour workday became the 12-hour workday, children became problematic and burdensome, which gave rise to daycare centers and providers—like myself.

Have women come a long way? You bet. Have they done really well evolving from servants to professionals? Very well, indeed, and at break-neck speed. But children have become lost in the mix. There has never been a good answer to the loss of mom from the home, and for sure, mom continues to be gone, for her world in America cannot function without her paycheck. And unfortunately, other cultural changes grabbed and yanked her into a self-obsession that is unmatched in history minus the kings, queens, pharaohs, dictators, and monarchs of days mostly gone by, minus, of course, the global elites. As America became obsessed with television and movie stars, somehow women glued themselves to TV's bandwagon and felt they deserved pure, unadulterated luxuries of the media elite. They felt entitled to every indulgence that could be named and purchased, and they didn't care what it cost. No price was too high to pay for celebrity-style living. And one other issue—women were no longer dependent on men. They could and can make it alone. It is interesting to me that all married women I know have said, should they ever find themselves single via divorce or death, they will never, ever remarry. It seems that men, to American women, have become somewhat unnecessary after children are born. In inordinately large numbers, women today find men, and particularly husbands, to be stupid, embarrassing, and lacking in purpose minus money. They find them to be shallow, boring companions, and childish. Remember that, historically, this is how men viewed women—shallow, boring, and childish. It seems as if we are in the midst of an old role reversal here in contemporary America. And it seems that many American women are rather sullen toward husbands. As a woman who did not choose wisely when it came to mates, I understand some of the disappointments. However, there are many wonderful men in the world, so I have to ask myself this question, "What has caused the great divide, the tremendous disrespect women feel toward men?"

Well, history exists and is certainly in the minds of women. They know their history, as a gender, has been loathsome. But it's more than this. There is something wrong at the core of the chasm between today's men and women, husbands and wives, and I think women are going to have to dig deeply to find answers.

Children need and want fathers. I, too, have toyed with the idea that this may not be true, and that fatherhood is simply a romanticized and historical norm that, until recently, was based on ownership. In reality, women have been raising children alone since the beginnings of time when fathers were killed on hunts, in wars, via plagues and diseases, and all other forms of demise. Women manage. But, on the other hand, men can and often do love their children. Men can and often do love their wives. And simply because American women have changed so radically in a very short period of time doesn't mean that men don't have critical roles to play in families. Men may not have to hunt the mammoth anymore, but that doesn't mean they don't want to.

Yes, women, we can laughingly say that men are stupid, boring, and embarrassing. I've said it myself, and to degrees, perhaps I've meant it at times, but I'm also now looking at you, who have lost your womanly arts skills, who have sub-contracted your children to me, who look and act like airbrushed posters, and all the while bankrupting your family for the sake and saving of your looks. Stupid is what stupid does, and you can't judge a gender lest you become what you loathe. Think about that. I suggest to women that if family does not come first, then loyalty, as a concept, cannot exist. Loyalty is bred in the family home.

The Compassionless Female

Compassion is what sets human beings apart. The ability to love may be the greatest virtue, but the ability to feel pain, sorrows, and sufferings of others, and to be able act on those feelings, makes us unique.

A doctor, who is the greatest technician in the world, is loathed if he is without compassion. A veterinarian without compassion is a freak. Religious leaders, responsible for the guiding of souls and spirits, and who are without compassion, are evil. Mothers, who bring children into the world, and who have no compassion for their children, are perhaps the most despicable human beings in all the world's societies. Almost nothing is more dreaded and loathed than mothers who have no compassion for their children. They are taboo. And yet, every mother knows that there are times, when overloaded by work, tiredness, anxiety, screaming children, and the hundred other problems that plaque people on any ordinary day – all mothers have let their compassion slip in fed-up moments. Mothers, after all, are human. But for most women of all cultures, compassion is inbred by nature. It exists and functions on its own. One would think that it would take millions of years for an innate ability to vanish, but in fact, culture can kill compassion, or its ability to operate, rapidly. Go to the soccer fields and watch feminine compassion fail.

Most women believe they are good mothers. Most never question the level of skill they've developed as primary nurturer. When their children are born, they hold, feed, clean, and clothe them; children grow and mothers love them and give them everything they can. They educate them and try to keep their children content, and mothers try to prepare children for adulthood. Again I say – maybe or maybe not.

According to a new Webster's dictionary, and also my favorite dictionary, *Webster's Revised Unabridged Dictionary of the English Language,* published in 1890, "compassion" means to literally suffer with another. It is the sensation of sorrow excited by the distress of another. Compassion is pity and it is merciful. This is why everyone hates a mother who murders her children. The thought of childhood death, at the hands of a mother, is unthinkable to people. It doesn't make biological sense, and it is as horrifying a crime as any can be. But what about the slow death of a child's spirit through neglect, lack of nutrition, lack of attention, and lack of physical, parental presence? Perhaps the child does not die in body, but what happens to a mind and soul too sad and lethargic to function?

Imagine, if you will, that your life is totally exposed to your neighbors—every intimate detail of your daily life. Every thing you do, every chore you perform, every phone call monitored, every shopping trip and spree monitored. Every word you say to your children and husband, every look on your face, every activity you engage in – morning, noon, and night—and every task you perform and thing you say to and about your family. Then imagine the movie version shown to every person on your street. Frightening, isn't it (and a very good reason to resist panoptical and chipping technologies)?

My premise is that mothers feel and are less compassionate toward their children in today's America. All mothers? No, but as the lavish life styles of stars are now the mainstream suburban habits of middle-class women, I think I can easily suggest that the focus of middle-class mothers has become themselves and not their children. As biological females, to have the ability to put mundane and self-serving desires above the basic needs of your children demonstrates that your compassion as biological females is really, really, really weak. I think of the stereotypical "Jewish mother," who has been made fun of for decades in the United States – the neurotically and overly-concerned mothers and their minute by minute doings, worrying, and lavishing of attention and time upon their children. It's interesting to me how well those children turn out to be in America's Jewish homes.

What is compassionate about women who are obsessed with their health and looks, and don't feed their children nutritious food? What compassionate mother would force a child to live in a sterile museum? What compassionate mother would leave a child in daycare for 10 to 12 hours a day – especially when she doesn't have a job? What kind of biological compassion screams at six-years-olds on soccer fields, and gives them hell publicly for their performances after games? And what kind of compassion demonstrates itself with television sets and computer games rather than, together, doing yard work, gardening, reading books, or baking cookies with children? And for that matter, what kind of compassion sends children into public schools, year after year, knowing full well that corruptions of every kind can and do infect them—especially the corruptions of Socialist union teachers and their political agendas?

Well, it's something to mill around. Our compassions for each other are the only true borders between barbarism and civility. You take away compassion from any human being, you create damage—pure, living damage whether it is to yourself or your children. And if you can honestly say that you have denied your children basic, primary compassions, then your claim to motherhood is a lie.

The Unfaithful Female

The cheating wife used to be rather rare, for the unfaithfulness of women, historically, has also been taboo. In many cultures and to this day, unfaithfulness by women can be grounds for death. In America, it has always been grounds for social contempt and scorn as women have always been held to higher standards of behavior than men. In public schools, for instance, they are still held to higher standards. Boys are continuously let off for rule breaking for "being boys." Sex crimes against women and children have been tolerated in America. They always have been. From time to time, the serial rapist or serial child molester serves life, but the usual time served for any sex crime is one or two years or less. As I said, there is still no national expectation for justice when it comes to violent crimes against women. And there is a lot of dust under this rug—mountains of it.

But today's women have changed. They can have babies and not marry at all. They can raise children with their individual incomes. They can date many men at once. And they can also cheat on husbands, and do. In fact, recent data suggests that women in marriage cheat at a rate nearing 50% versus 80% for cheating husbands. And the divorce rate is 50/50? I guess that's not so bad considering the cheating stats.

Interestingly, many women talk about their infidelities with friends, laugh about affairs, and seem to enjoy, like men, living with secrets. Their adultery is for the public enjoyment of some, as has typically been the case with men and their male confidants. As previously stated, be careful you don't become what you loathe...

In my old fashioned sensibilities, the double standard rears its ugly head. I don't like the idea of women cheating on husbands. It's the same travesty, same sin as men cheating on wives, but I expect a more spiritual AND maternal consideration of consequences from women. We are not led by our vaginas. Women are led by stable home lives, children, and the need for a protected nest. Extra-marital affairs are not led by love or children waiting to be emotionally and socially wrecked by marital indiscretions. In fact, women who cheat, to this reader, are insidious. So many of us know the pain, so why would we inflict it upon our children and the men we marry. Call me sexist, but I do hold women to a higher standard when it comes to children – the highest standard, for if mothers fail, children fall. If fathers fail, children are damaged, but can and do recover with a strong mother. And I may as well say what will surely not sit well with some: Women are more equipped to be the primary nurturer. We come with breasts and with bodies that grow children. I believe, therefore, that we are simply more equipped for childcare and raising children. If you toy with this biology in order to have affairs—I'm sorry but you are one sorry woman because this type of behavior will cause your children irrefutable, emotional damage. The bonds of trust and nurturing between mother and children absolutely must be set in stone. If you betray your children, lie to your children about your devotion to their health, happiness, their fathers, and futures, then you are rotten at heart. Ouch…the truth always hurts somebody. Again—if there is no loyalty to family, no loyalties of any kind can exist.

It is my opinion that many women cheat for revenge or simply because they can. We are free. We can do what we want when we want…but some things are cheap entitlements—really stupid, cruel, and cheap. However, in today's world, cheating is vogue and quietly accepted. Many, many women suck up the pain and pretend that their marriages are fine when husbands cheat. They feel that airing dirty laundry is socially condemning, so they, in effect, help the cheating husband to hide and continue the disloyalty. But cheating wives seem to enjoy affairs on several levels. They often think affairs are funny and to be bragged about. They seem to actually gain self-esteem. And excuse me for such audacity, but some of the current TV shows, which turn adultery into comedy viewing at prime time, are literally dangerous to women. And I pray to God that no child watches these shows, though, in fact, they demonstrate, to perfection, much of the material in this book. TV…great cultural documentation and hypnosis.

Well, I've identified that cheating women are in style. I'll let my daycare children finish up this chapter:

"Mommy has a man friend. I saw them kissing."

"Mom likes Mr. Henley. She invites him over when Dad goes to Boston."

"I'm not allowed in Mommy's room when Mr. Eric comes over. He brings me presents."

"Mommy and our neighbor are dirty. They take baths together."

The Unwell Spirit aka Hypochondria

I personally know a young woman who goes to herbologists, chiropractors, a general practitioner, a gynecologist, a massage therapist, an internal medicine specialist, a plastic surgeon, an orthopedic surgeon, a psychologist, and an endocrinologist. And she is healthy as a horse. However, she is bored with her life, does not have a job, contracts her children out to several nannies, and has a permanent gardener and two handymen. She also has several interior decorators, two maids, window washers, and a score of laborers to maintain her houses. She has absolutely nothing to do because she sub-contracted herself right out of purpose and meaning. Consequently, she is very depressed but has mistaken her depression for death knocking at her door. She also believes herself to be horribly over worked. When I talk to her, I literally end up being speechless – I don't know what to say because her delusions are not just delusions. They are her entire life. She has systematically removed all meaning from her existence. I end up shaking my head, agreeing with everything she says, and walking away in a daze. And what I now realize is that delusional lives are being lived everywhere in America, and they have become the norm for whole communities of women. This life style used to be reserved for the extremely wealthy and busy movers and shakers of the world. However, via envy and greed, middle-class women are now mimicking this mode of living. And you ask why medical insurance costs are out of control...

I know soccer moms, with two or more children, who go to massage therapists, chiropractors, day spas, and psychologists every week. And they pay for childcare, maid service, and lawn service every week. And they don't have jobs. Again, I find myself without words, but I guarantee you, I'll think of a few as I mull this phenomenon over in my mind.

To begin with, the annual cost of all this must simply be beyond all comprehension, and it serves one person in the entire family – one. It also demonstrates women as total incompetents—unable to even run a sweeper or wash a dish. In fact, women lower themselves to little more than someone else's bills. They generate cost to the family but contribute absolutely nothing. They become, themselves, bills to pay. Now I understand the term "high maintenance women."

Next, imagine being a child with a mother who does nothing in the home but is always off to doctors, therapists, to massage appointments, beauty parlors, shopping, movies, luncheons, and more doctors. How does this child define the word "mother."? A gorgeous shopper who is going to drop dead any minute? And then imagine this mother telling her child that she is overworked and exhausted. Shall we call this warping the child's view of reality and parenthood? And how does this child emotionally connect to a mother who is always gone or unwell? And I hear this stuff every day on the soccer sidelines where women complain and moan about their health and spa appointments because they simply have so little time and are so tired to begin with. What can a normal human being say about this? How did women get to be so absurd? Why do they choose sickness over function, sickness over purpose? Let's at least attempt to make some sense of how this mental illness came to be.

In all countries throughout history, slaves and middle-class people have been the backbones of cultures. They have been the worker bees, the inventors, the artists, the frugal, the prudent—the true builders of culture. With the sweat of their labors in homes and at work, and with their family values and belief systems, they created communities, cities, countries and cultural norms, mores, and values. The kings and queens, monarchs and pharaohs, and even religious leaders were always set apart. They were the few though they made the rules and insisted that their whims be served. They were the few because the rest of mankind did the work and built the world. The middle-class, especially, have always has been the rock of humanity. And middle-class families have always been known for their devotion to the family. This has been the history of the world. But again, here in America, where leadership likes to change things as rapidly as possible, modernize, and evolve into desired entities, we now have a middle-class who believes they are upper class and deserve upper-class luxuries and livings. And they are becoming as biased and corrupt as "leadership" has mostly been. We should also make note that the middle-class have always been the ones to dismantle cultures that were too cruel, selfish, or brutal to stand. That was because they were the strongest, had the most fortitude, and therefore made the best soldiers. But America's middle-class is fast changing. They are losing strength in many, many ways.

Economically, most American people are essentially broke from materialistic debt, the Federal Reserve, and corporately imposed inflation. Half of their marriages have ended in divorce. As workers, they are half blue-collar and half white-collar, which means they know how to do half as much with their hands. Most can't and don't grow food, can't fix cars or small machinery or household machines, and most are one to two paychecks from poverty and two to three months from homelessness. Half or more of their children live with one parent or the other, and at least half of middle-class men pay or owe enormous child support payments. However, one would never know that the middle-class is broke by looking at its women.

Today's middle-class females shower themselves with every luxury that money can buy. They live in expensive and very large houses and drive terribly expensive and gas guzzling automobiles. They have diamond jewelry, designer clothing, designer sunglasses, designer furniture, and designed landscapes. They have maids and other servants. They are living according to their role models, which are celebrities of every make and flavor. And still, with all this self-lavishing and adornment, women want and seem to need even more attention, and they seek it out in medical communities whereby they continue to talk even more and at length about themselves. Every ache and pain becomes a crisis. Every blue moment becomes a breakdown. Every sore muscle becomes so important that even it needs its own masseuse, orthopedic surgeon, and chiropractor. And every upset in the home needs a psychotherapist. Hypochondria is the icing on the cake of self-obsession and self-deification. And so to stay sick breeds more and more focused attention upon the pathologically bored, insecure, and needy female. She would rather be sick than normal, for normality draws no interest or special attention. So in great numbers, hypochondria has become vogue among middle-class women. Seeing therapists is a sign of prosperity. Running to multiple doctors is something to do and provides a captive audience whereby women can talk about nothing at all but themselves. So, the question is—what are we really looking at here? Why are women in droves doing the sickness thing?

Here's my guess: I think middle-class women are being eaten alive, from the inside out, with guilt – pure and unadulterated guilt. I think they know they are guilty of poor mothering, being poor and mean-spirited wives, being bloodthirsty spendthrifts, and self-worshipping. I think they are shame-ridden by their shallowness and rejection of womanhood. But I think that the "play rich" trends have become over-powering and far-reaching. Too many women have rooted themselves to the lifestyle and fear the loss of social status, gossip, and rumors. You can see how skewed priorities have become as women choose status and appearances over family, and pathetically, many, many women are now depressed, manic, and diagnosable.

I think these women long for peace and safety and are simply caught up in what may be the dumbest worldliness ever known, and I think, deep down, they feel like fools. I think their spirits are suffering under the unbearable weights of debt, impossible perfections, social tunnels whereby with one step off the beaten path you can and will land in Shun City, and with one more angry and unreasonable explosion of temper, they fear their husbands will walk out and never come back. I think there is a collective unwellness in the spirits of many, many American women, and I think it's a completely solvable problem. I believe that the self-inflicted burdens and mental pressures can be removed with truth.

It hurts to have to prove lies. It's hard to do. The pressures are too great and lies layer one on another on another. You are not upper class. You do not have a lot of money. You are not wealthy. You cannot afford the house you live in or the car that you drive. You cannot afford day spas or nails or tanning or cosmetologists or weekly hair appointments or psychologists or maids or landscapers or window cleaners. You can barely afford groceries, the power and electric bills, and the phone bill. You're in credit card trouble and your cable bill costs too much. Your husband doesn't like you very much and you're worried that he's seeing some else because he comes home late all the time. You actually can't stand your friends because they are shallow, snobby, gossiping, mean, and conniving women. They never, ever have really done anything for you except allow you to be seen with them. And you feel unwell because you are so stressed by the appearances you feel forced to keep and by the sheer debt of perfections of all kinds. And you have neglected your children day after day, year after year, and you know it, and you have blamed them for your neglect. And you have spent and spent and spent to recreate your image and, internally, you don't like the image you've created because it is not you at all and it's still not good enough. And your spirit is sad and tired, and you've forgotten what a good person you thought you once were. You've forgotten your dreams of a happy family and children and marriage. And equally, you've forgotten your personal dreams. And you feel empty at the core of your being. And your house is a burden and provides no comfort to anyone. And it is truth—just plain and simple truth—that will heal your sadness and the pain of your children and husbands. You got caught on a runaway train, and it's a wake-up call to your spirit. A healthy spirit does not get caught because it sees clearly and has a direction of its own. And it doesn't need perfections of any kind. It doesn't need contrived and manufactured beauty. It only needs the simplicity of truth and the gentleness of giving, and with just these two wonderful things, the spirit is healthy and knows where to turn when times get tough. It really is just this simple. Begin with the truth about your lives and regain your health and joy. You are not sick. You're just suffering beneath the unbearable weight of cultural-corporate lies.

Weight! There's More!

The women who bring their children to me and tell me never to give them cookies or candy or sugar of any kind are clearly, themselves, on diets. It's sad because I don't not know any women who are not on chronic diets. So, let's talk diets. It's an unavoidable subject when discussing women, as American females could, at any moment in time, be renamed diets.... not female, not mothers or wives or ladies or women with names...just...diets.

Where do we begin? Let's start in schools. Beginning around 2nd grade, or the age of seven or eight, girls begin hearing the sexual innuendos of boys. At the same time, they begin fascinations with make-up, dress-up, and womanly ways modeled by their mothers and television. It's the pre pre-pubescent stage. By the time they are nine or ten, the full-blown fascination with womanly ways has kicked in. All girls this age have, or get a hold of, nail polish, pink lipsticks, and they become interested in their hair. Equally, they enter the early stages of puberty and also notice, talk about, and get crushes on boys. Boys elevate their sexual commentary and innuendo as puberty wraps around their brains and manners. By age seven or eight, if a girl is over weight, her self-esteem has already been destroyed in school, and by age 10, her soul is permanently damaged through cruelty, public commentary of her body, humiliation, and self-loathing. She will suffer for the rest of her life and particularly throughout the rest of her school career and tormenting. Her teenage life in school will be a daily, living nightmare.

Now let's see what our culture says about women and their weight. In America, thinness is health and beauty. Average weights are 10 to 30 pounds overweight to the hypercritical American eye, and fatness is monstrous and grotesque. For men, thinness is wimpy, average is average, and fatness is not discussed except by the men themselves or doctors. There are many, many, many Hollywood male stars, athletes, and otherwise famous men who are overweight and very, very attractive and even sexy. Our culture, once again, continues to be unreasonably hard on women. In fact, it prefers women to remain girls who do not grow into women at all. Ideal American beauty is 15 to 18-years-old. Once past 18, she's teetering on womanhood, which is the beginning of the end of her "perfect" years. Magazines, television, the fashion industry, the sex-based youth culture, the make-up industry, and yes, schools, have retired American beauty at the age of about 20. I think this has sunk into women like lead and made has them crazy for decades – about four or five decades and certainly for the last three generations. Women compelled to compete with teenagers for desirability destroy their self-esteem in the very process. Equally, it makes mothers resentful of daughters and daughters distrusting and ashamed of mothers. And is it not telling that many American women shave their pubic hairs in order to look like children? Think about that. And another female problem is created – the feeling within girls that they, too, must compete with mothers for "beauty." Most female children attempt their first diets around the age of nine or ten, and some even earlier. They just diet right along side their mothers. Many pubescent girls work out with their mothers, and many girls are handed diet supplements from mothers and doctors. Kids have also been given diet camps in every state in the country.

Can we at least consider that we have been hoodwinked on top of disrespected? Can we not see that we have been bought by beauty entities and fallen like fools into corporate marketing traps? Or do we truly believe that we are so ugly and undesirable as females that we will go to any expense, through any pain, and any humiliation to be younger, thinner, and more artificial than to be our selves? And will we impose this cultural travesty upon the souls of our daughters and grand daughters? Will we pay for their plastic surgeries proving that we, too, find them as unattractive and imperfect as our culture finds us? When are we going to look in our mirrors and believe we are good enough? Not until we can will the culture even attempt to follow. Once again, we have done this to ourselves; we permitted the invasion of our bodies and souls by entities, and have become deadened in heart and mind. This is surely the saddest and most pathetic chapter in this book.

The Shallow Well

Perhaps my biggest beef with today's middle-class women—soccer moms, McMansion moms, day-spa moms, and female spenders has to do with their communications with each other. I see and hear women, every day, enveloped in two primary types of discussion: the back stabbing of others and senseless, social climbing projects. In fact, I hear almost no other topics of conversations whatsoever. This bothers me quite a bit, and concerns me further that women are declining intellectually and in depth.

My mother, who was a housewife, was perhaps the most well read woman I ever met. She could discuss any subject, any topic, with intellectual input and insights. She kept up, so to speak, with history, science, and current events, and she developed the kind of wisdoms that come with long-term thinking, historical knowledge, and considerations. She was not judgmental about politics, religion, history, or culture, but was intelligent by an enormous body of life-long study of humans and their developments throughout time. She was fascinating to talk to and everyone loved to be in her company because she was so interesting. She had perspective and was always interested in the opinions and perspectives of others. She was a fascinated person and hence, became fascinating as a woman of heart and mind. Since her death, I've been hard pressed to find other women of her intellectual stature, though I've found highly educated women everywhere. However, I'm far more likely to discuss house decorating, workout routines, or diets with these women. They don't seem capable of subject matter apart from themselves. And I can honestly say that many, many women spend the bulk of their conversations with other women in the crucifixion of other people or in the constant planning stages of self-rewarding. Sometimes, I sit and listen at the soccer fields, and I literally want to scream.

While history silenced our collective brainpower for centuries, now women sit and collectively rot their brains with mundane, foolish, and mean-spirited thoughts. And I see husbands sitting next to them for two hours and never speaking one word or even looking at their wives. They are embarrassed, and they are silent and distant with magazines and girl watching.

Today's women tend to make sport of trashing and gossiping about other women and children. They literally invent stories and suspicions and spread them throughout their peer groups and then return to their interior decorators, their purchases, and their health and beauty regimens. And when the poor soul who they've just lambasted walks by, they all say, and I quote, "...hello...how are you..." with bored intonations, and they smile and look away and to each other once the soul has passed by. And they feel superior while their cruelty is as public and visible as their blinding teeth. And their silence is horrendous when the soul, once more, walks near.

I don't get it. It has to do with social stature, with shunning those who they sense to be less, but less than what? Again I ask, what has happened to average women in America? They are incessantly judgmental and at the same time, as unaccomplished, uninspired, and useless as they have ever been in human history. They talk incessantly of themselves and of positively childish projects. And they do not talk about work, if they work. They are so emotionally snagged upon themselves that they are hateful toward most others, and this is really, really scary because they are also mothers. And I see the results of their classism clearly in their children. More quotes from the daycare:

"Mommy says that Rachel's mom is trash."
"Mom says that I can't play with my friend because her house is trashy."
"Mommy says I have to be a cheerleader so I have nice friends."
"Mommy says you have cheap clothes."
"Mom says her friend is a slut."
"Mom says we can only be friends with the kids in our neighborhood."
"Mommy says Black people are weird. What's Black people?"
"Mommy says the boy who sits next to me in school is bad."
"Mommy says {name} doesn't know how to decorate."
"Mom says { name's } dad is a loser."

I hear it all the time—that mother's crucify other people and impose their opinions upon their children. And these kids believe every word and begin their judgments at very young ages. Unfortunately, they take those judgments into the schools and tell their fellow students whom to persecute. There are children all over American schools who never have a chance, from day one, due to the undue influence of gossiping mothers and their mimicking children. It's awful. It's cruelty in tremendous numbers, and again, very public for listening pleasures on every soccer field in the country. It's beyond awful. It's beyond gossip. It's perpetration with intent to permanently divide. It's unadulterated class war.

In large numbers, it is becoming vogue for middle-class women to be cruel, dividing, and mean-spirited. It has become, in fact, socially acceptable and mandated in the circles of women who see themselves as upper class, though they are, in reality, middle-class. They are so diluted that their intellects are literally dying. They don't even know their socio-economic levels. And I say this: you can't cover stupidity and cruelty with all the make-up and bleach in the world. Your children will grow to be ghastly people and your husbands, if they have backbones, will leave you. Your horrible behaviors will leave generational wakes of judgments and unkindness and hatreds between normal, average people—what you are – no more, no less. And how did you come to the collective conclusion that group lynching was your means to exclusiveness and superiority? It's positively bizarre.. Granted – extreme wealth has always claimed exclusivity, but you are middle class, average women who contribute just about nothing to society. On what is your superiority based? Your fully loaded credit cards? Your large, cheaply build houses? Your blinding teeth?

Shallow wells dry up. Deep wells provide for the long term. And no one, including your children, will want you when you're old, homely, and mean in spirit. Worst-case scenario? They will become you and as worthless as you became.

The Divorced Child

"Children of divorce" is a wimpy phrase. It is meant to skim the devastation and, at the same time, offer clinical, social condolences to children from divorced families. Since half (and I suspect many more than half) of America's children are from broken marriages, let's admit that the subject deserves honest consideration and perhaps some unsterilized truth about what really happens to children of divorced parents in America.

First, Americans will divorce for any and all reasons. We don't even need to mention the three or four good reasons to divorce because, minus violence, they are the rare exception nowadays. In fact, the number one reason for divorce in America today is "incompatibility."

Incompatibility is a very long word. Let's shorten it to its actual meaning in divorce court—boredom. More marriages in the United States end in boredom than for any other reason. It is the number one cause of divorce according to statistics, citing that 60% of all divorces in America end due to "incompatibility." And it's funny how you can witness the impending collapse of a marriage by watching and listening to the participating adults. The term "whatever" is frequently heard. The phrases "...I guess..." and "..do what ever you want..." are hints that lawyers are impending. It's interesting that two people can love each other, be obsessed with each other, think of nothing but each other, make plans to marry and be the happiest people on the planet – and one year later feel like maybe...And two years later be bored stiff with the other person in the bed. And three years later are suing for custody, child support, and alimony because the person has become so evil and mentally incompetent that he/she should be disallowed, by law, all contact with his/her children.

Okay. I can hear the, yes, but what ifs...now. Sure, there are the exceptions. But boredom is still the number one cause of divorces in the U.S. of A., and that's a statistical fact.

Women initiate most divorce proceedings, and I don't believe it's because many men cheat. I think women leave marriages because they are unhappy and bored. I'm not saying that anyone should stay in an unhappy and boring marriage. I just think we should begin in an honest place. American women do not like boredom. Over shopping, over grooming, and self-lavishing demonstrates this—clearly. We have all grown in a culture that is entertainment-oriented. Boredom has become a mental illness in our culture, and we need to acknowledge this, as well. Bored American women get silent (a sure sign of trouble) and bitchy. We get itchy for change. We are a product of our culture and we enjoy "newness" just as America enjoys newness. It is our culture's unique phenomenon and curse.

Men, I believe, enjoy stability more than women. They function well within reliable patterns. Dinner at about the same time, Sunday and Monday football, grass cutting on Saturday mornings, kids in bed at 8:30 p.m., shower at 6:00 a.m., a wife who is home before he gets home, news at 11:00 p.m., bed at 11:30 p.m., and job – 7:00 a.m. to 6:00 p.m., Monday through Friday. Women cannot adhere to this schedule or else they go mad. I believe women need fluctuations as their minds are more complexly wired. I believe women are vulnerable to boredom and in fact add deviations to their days in order to keep their minds stimulated. In fact, I'd guess that the routine-driven man and the deviation-driven female is a formula for the no-fault divorce. Add to that the middle-class's now prevalent and expensive entertainment and spending habits, and the formula for divorce is practically perfect. Bored woman, insecure man, and both flat broke? See you in court.

Divorce is a legal right in America, and I, personally, am very grateful for that right. But, as with other rights in our country, children often suffer at the hands of adult freedoms.

Catholics, for the most part, don't believe in divorce. Actually, I don't know anyone who believes in divorce. That's like saying I don't believe in drivers' licenses. In America, marriage has become clinical. It may start as romance and love full of life-long dreams, but in reality, marriage is TV – you can have one or not. Marriage used to be based upon religious principles. It is still mostly an arrangement sworn to in churches, synagogues, temples, and to God, but most do not take marriage this seriously in the United States. It's a ceremonious party, where tons and tons of money is spent, and with a great vacation at the end of the party. Then the reality of the marriage kicks in when newlyweds begin the process of cost analysis, children, and day-to-day tasks and functions of adults. Suddenly, marriage is not based on the Divine but in bills, laundry, kids, and the daily habits of the man in the tuxedo and the woman in the gown that you saw once—as if in a dream. Suddenly, the spiritual uniting as one becomes the buffoon at the computer and the bitch on the couch. The Holy union is out and the individual parties, with their wants and agendas, challenge each other for power and opportunity. The man burrows into his cultural definitions as husband and provider, and the woman becomes judgmental of the routines of her husband and children. She feels trapped in the boredom of expectations. In today's world, she is also very, very sensitive about being seen or used as family servant, and she is unprepared for the stress of cooking, cleaning, and child rearing when she was trained, in childhood, for dating, beauty, college, and career. Women, too, have become disrespectful of domesticity, and yet they are also self, culturally, and biologically programmed to be good mothers, wives, and homemakers. The problem is, they are not filling these roles, and women feel incompetent coming or going.

If she is a career woman, she worries about her children being raised and cared for by others, and she's tired once home. She doesn't want to be Martha Stewart, and yet chaos breaks loose every weeknight around 6:00 p.m., when dinner, homework, baths, youth sports, and husbands look to her for traditional womanhood. Frankly, it's practically a no-win situation. One wonders if America also clashes with the traditional family. It's no wonder that marriage has less than a 50/50 chance.

And its no wonder so many children suffer in marriages that have no meaningful foundations. Children can't thrive when parents are competitive, uncooperative, and disrespectful toward each other. Children can't thrive with parents who are at odds with opinions and embroiled in power struggles. And when divorce becomes reality, children do pick sides because, ultimately, they must. They will be primarily the charge of one parent or the other, or they will be literally split in half for their livings – as in "shared parenting."

Divorce is nothing more or less than war in microcosm. But the war is the country, religion, economic base, and social universe of the child. The war causes the destruction of everything the child knows in his or her culture. It is the child's world war, for the world of the child, and everything in it, dies. And the victim of the war is the divorced child.

By virtue of the battlefield, the child will pick a side to stay alive and sane. One parent or the other becomes suspect and eventually, the bad guy. Someone will transform from the loving mother or father into the guilty destroyer. Who that person is depends on the wrathful strength of one or the other parent. Who will win the communication battle to convince the child of the other's terrorism? Ultimately, the objective will be to win physical custody and the future of the child. The true agenda will be, "Will my child be like him or me?" Ultimately, the child will choose which parent to divorce, and in effect, will halve himself, his psyche, and soul.

All people, including children, want to be on the winning side. So they divorce one parent and become more akin to the other. They pull back from one and become vulnerable to the other's impending lifestyle to come. The child actually becomes a conquered nation. And as a conquered entity in a war, the child grows with resentments, fears, angers, and an inability to trust. The child becomes internally sad as all conquered peoples are in the losing of their histories and culture, and the affects of loss and culture last for generations. So let's say, for now, that a good analogy for the divorced child is the history of Native American people: conquered, helpless, angry, untrusting, poor, sad, stripped of their culture and history, and totally vulnerable to conquerors and their decisions.

Divorced children are fundamentally sad people. They remind me of every Native American I've ever met. There is a deep sadness in their eyes and souls that is so visible and profound, that one cannot help but to soulfully cringe knowing what has happened—knowing the generational layers of themselves that have been stripped and stolen away.

But parents don't consider this in their boredoms. They don't care enough about their children and what it means to destroy, in total, their entire world. I live with this every day as my children bear the trademark sadness in their eyes. Now I know it's permanent. I ask that you consider your choices in the world of your children. I ask you to put your children above your boredoms. If you are incompatible with your mate, remember that people change, and that you will not be the same at 20 as you will be at 30 and 40. Be careful with your children's souls. And think about this: we now divorce far more easily and readily due to boredom than unfaithfulness or even battery. Upwards of 50% of American children, today, have had their worlds torn in half because one or both of their parents were incompatible, bored, and ready for something or someone new. Think about it – choosing pain inflicted upon your children over boredom. I suggest you need a better reason than this.

The Single American Mom

I know a lot about this subject for I have raised two daughters mostly alone and for 34 years. I've been both a horrible mother and a good mother. Both were learning experiences primarily on the spiritual level, for both of my children, and my struggles to raise them, made me a smarter and more decent human being. My gratitude to them is beyond words. My desire for their forgiveness is far greater.

Over half of American children are from broken marriages, and mothers raise 90% of those children. What can I say about single motherhood? It's hard. Sickness is not an option for a single mother. There is no time to get sick, and if you do become ill, you keep going and ignore it. Boredom is not an option – there is no time for boredom. Money is always tight. Vacations are a rarity. My last vacation was in 1992, and four days long. But I can deal with this and have. However, what makes me very angry about single motherhood is that I am a second-class citizen. I am less than a married mother, less than a married couple, and far less in the eyes of expert American "cultural" professionals.

I'm told I am a poor mother. I'm told that my children are problems to society, in schools, and in their adulthoods. I am repeatedly told that I am not enough by myself, or good enough or competent enough to raise an intellectually, emotionally, or spiritually healthy child. I can and do take issue with this. I don't like it at all, though in fact, and as I've said, my children bare the trademark sadness in their eyes of fatherless children. So, I willingly think it through though I also carry my barrage of weapons on the road to this consideration. This is a touchy subject on a thousand levels. Let's begin simply with the American history of "the single adult female" or "spinster."

It has been an unkind history. Too ugly to marry, to stupid, less than good enough to be someone's wife—single, adult women have never been prized in America but rather women of pity; the women unwanted by men. Hmmm.

Add to this the woman who became pregnant while unmarried. Then she is sinful and grossly unwanted by men and society. She is a bad seed with bastard in tow. Now the fathers of these children were, and very often continue to be, scott-free and not responsible in any way, while the women are branded for life, eecking out difficult and lonely livings for themselves and their children – while constantly, continually judged and shunned. Their children fare no better. Spinsters and single mothers have always been mistreated and disrespected in America. Those Puritanical judgments carried through time.

What is odd is to me is how, during the 1960's and 70's, culture swung hard-left and a youth-based culture decided that sex would be casual, public, and fun. Bizarrely, it took root in contemporary culture. We went from a rigid, Puritanical base to a total turn-around in sexual mores. And it took hold everywhere and is now, even with AIDS, normal. Casual sex has become mainstream with both kids and adults. Kids "hook up," 80% of husbands cheat, and boys, for sport, have sex as often as they can with as many as they can. It has been this way for upwards of 50 years now – 50 years! Is sexual casualness wrong? That's what I've heard most of my life, but it's worse now than it was when I was a young woman – much worse and far more widespread. So, culturally, we accepted casual sex. We can't say it isn't so, because, clearly, it is so. I refer you to prime time TV. It's wrong, of course. We all know it, sense it, feel it in our bones and read it in all scriptures, but "the culture" has accepted sex as sport. Adolescent and pre-adolescent boys talk about it openly in every classroom and on every school bus in America, and no one even attempts to curb them. Girls are bombarded in schools, on a daily basis, with sexual innuendo and commentary, and there are no repercussions, whatsoever, though plenty of cover-ups. We know this, too, and yet we send our female children into schools every day.

Sexual misconduct is hand-smacked in our courtrooms. Rapists are rarely chased by authorities unless they are high-profile cases or criminals, and child molesters are hand-smacked with kid gloves in America. Sexual misconduct, sex crimes, and sexual harassment are swept under rugs and hushed up. And most of these crimes are perpetrated upon women. So I contend that there is still commonplace and fundamental disrespect for women in America. There has yet to be any national expectation that women will be respected or legally treated. To me, it's confounding and utterly unbelievable, but it's also a historical American pattern.

Now, American is full of divorced people. More than half of all marriages are dumped and more than half of all American children are divorced. Single mothers who, so sadly and wrongly, remain absolutely disrespected by American culture raise 90% of divorced children. Maybe it's just me, but I see a real problem here and it's an old, old problem. Women still take the cultural heat for sex crimes against them, unwanted pregnancy, and unwanted children. And single mothers are also unwanted and unaccepted in the world of the married—again, an old, old pattern.

Single mothers in America seem to come in two flavors: really, really good parents or really, really bad parents. It's not surprising. One overcompensates and the other doesn't even try. Neither is this surprising for the task borders on the impossible. It's no wonder so many single mothers just quit trying to do it all and let their children run through the culture like alley cats. So many single moms are unaided in any way and so shunned to boot, that they simply try to keep working, put food on the table, attempt to keep their kids in school, pay the bills on time, and collapse each and every night in their lack of support and community. They just try to keep it all going – champions that they are. And when their kids succumb to some cultural travesty, they just pray for the best because they are soulfully burned out.

The over-compensator just has more stamina. She tries everything to keep her children happy, healthy, and safe. But her vulnerability to failure is just one bad influence away from her children, and she knows that cultural odds are not in her favor. But she keeps at it for her children.

In my daycare experience, I've found that the children of single mothers are also two-folded: fantastic kids and terribly needy kids. I have so many memories of these children, but I will offer just a few of their comments for consideration:

"My mom is the best mom in the world!"
"My mom is never home. She has two jobs"
"My mom says I'm the smartest person she ever knew."
"I have to go to another baby-sitter when I'm sick."
"Me and mommy do everything together. She's my best friend."
"I don't have any friends because mommy sleeps all the time and I'm not allowed to go outside."

So there they are – the single mothers and their children. It's better to have two parents... better for everyone, but the single mother is special because her life is more difficult than anyone can imagine. And it is just incomprehensible to me that she continues to be a lesser person in this culture; that professionals and media malign her, she is shunned by married people, and still looked down upon in general. She is the bravest of the brave and the strongest woman of all. Befriend the single mother. Learn her world and put a personal stop to her cruel and inhumane misjudgment, for when you shun her, you also shun her children and purposefully. It's bad history, and it's way past time to set it straight.

Part II – The Culture

The Truth About Males & Females by Anti-Experts

One day, my daughter asks, "Mom, why are boys so stupid?" Well, this conversation began one evening in the car and ended the following evening. This is an example of how females are willing to talk things thoroughly through, taking the time needed to deliberate an important issue. We talked it over, offered examples from our experiences, and I'm happy to say, we decided that men were not stupid. The fact that they are not females sometimes confuses stupidity with maleness, and our conclusions, the more we came to them, were simply right on the money. So via the experience of a 52-year-old female, whose marriages have failed, and the experiences of a girl and her observations of boys, we offer the unprofessional following:

It is our premise that while females multi-task every minute of their waking lives, men uni-task. Once again, as we have performed every duty of our lives throughout human history with children in tow, we were simply biologically required to be capable of performing 20 functions at the same time. This remarkable ability gave rise to minds that were also capable of having multiple conversations and thoughts at once – hence, our social-ness and talkativeness. However, angered women tend to layer angers. As they hold much in their minds at one time, they also can unload layers and layers of angers in one fell swoop.

When we thought of what annoys men and boys about females, we realized that what men consider to be "yapping and yapping" is actually the female brain in its purest form of delivery and expression. Women can hear 20 conversations at once and understand them. Listen to a room full of women. They can and do talk about children, husbands, houses, jobs, volunteer projects, grandparents, and five other subjects in the course of two minutes while, at the same time, are straightening up, changing diapers, cooking, watering plants, feeding pets, serving food, answering emails, and talking on the phone. This ability is impossible and totally lost on men. They hear "yapping" because their brains can't take in floods of rapid thoughts in conversation. In fact, when faced with rapid, multiple conversations, men literally shut it out. We've all seen this ten thousand times. They go to another room or to the TV. They go outside and cut grass. They go to the basement and do just about anything to avoid having their brains stressed by the constant activity, volume, and talking of females. And this is especially true for men who are faced with the multi-tasking anger of a woman. They typically leave or explode.

Unfortunately, women mistake the uni-tasking male for stupid, disinterested, or bored, and men mistake the multi-tasking female for crazy, bitchy, and controlling. The truth, however, is that biology, nature, God, whatever your preference, developed our brains very differently, and we continue to beat each other over the heads with these differences. We're really, really late in thinking this through and understanding our differences intelligently. Yes, there have been books and programs about the uniqueness of men and women, but it's really a very simple issue. We are not the same because our brains are not the same. And once again, children are at the very root and heart of the matter. Women's communication, language, and mode of expression is all a result of motherhood, and that, my friends, is what defines us as female. And our female-ness does not set us apart from men. That's cultural stuff. It, however, defines what we do, how we do it, and certainly, how we say it.

My daughter and I came to another conclusion during our day of discussing men. We realized that having had 10-hour a day contact with children for years and years, we identified patterns common to little boys, such as the following:

- Little boys perform pretend-falling-down ritual for females.
- Little boys build lego figures for females.
- Little boys need to hear that females are pleased with their projects.
- Little boys tell females about their talents.
- Little boys frequently check to see where females are in the house.
- Little boys frequently touch or lean upon females.

In conclusion, we realized that little boys require close proximity to females. They don't want it – they need it, and equally, little boys perform for females and want their admiration. And this, my sisters in modern culture, is also the case for adult men. Men need women to be pleased with them on multiple levels and as a general rule. In truth, men intuitively know that women's brainpower is at least far more complex than theirs. Knowing so, men need reassurance that their abilities are needed and that they please women. They need to be intellectually respected by women and truly desire their focus and attention.

In today's America, where women can function with or without men, a fundamental need in males has been taken away and men are wounded. It is why they make fun of those who call themselves feminists. It is why they insult women casually with other men. It is why, at times, they grow to hate women and become violent toward them. It is at the core of a rage-filled divorce, because at the core of their being, which is their gender, and their very natures and instincts as males, they have become culturally unnecessary to females. And they are left without primary definitions as men. And the lack of definition creates a dangerous world for women and children. As I've said before, men without definition are wild, violent and, yes, stupid. They always have been and will continue to be, because that's the nature of the male being. If they are unneeded and undefined by their place with women and children, they can be dangerous and stupid. Women know this. So do girls. Gangs of young men and boys, without a defined and purposeful distraction of females with their biological agendas and goals, are unstoppable in their potential stupidities. It doesn't make women better or smarter. The two genders, together, civilize each other to a larger extent than when alone. When paired, male to female, women are less chaotic, nervous and vulnerable, and men are simply more civilized. This isn't rocket science. You don't need a manual. That about covers it.

Before I end this chapter, I have to relay to you the funniest story about a man that I've ever heard in my life. My sister, who is a doctor, told me this wonderful tale about her husband—a brilliant, well-read, and educated man who is a surgeon and originally from Germany. This story is the classic analogy of the differences between the male and female minds, their ways of doing things, and their responses to each other:

My sister's husband, we'll call him Conrad, was observed sweeping crumbs on the kitchen table into a pile with his hands. He went around to each corner of the table and methodically brushed each and every crumb into a pile in the middle of the table. After he had assembled his pile of crumbs, he brushed the pile carefully, meticulously, and neatly to the edge of the table whereby, he then pushed all the crumbs off the edge of the table and onto the floor.

There were two female observers in the room, his wife and adult daughter. They watched him gathering his crumbs. They would have done that job differently, but it was okay – he was helping. But the crumb brushing was taking a very long time and their curiosity and fascination was building. They looked at each other frequently with wide eyes. They folded their arms across their chests and continue to watch the piling of the crumbs. My sister glanced at her wall clock. Her daughter blew on her eyeglasses and wiped the lenses with her shirttail. This was the most thorough and longest job of crumb gathering in the history of the world. And then, to their abject horror and shock, Conrad swept his pile of crumbs off the table and onto the floor. Conrad then went to the sink to get a drink of water and sat down at the clean table.

"...WHAT....WHAT...WHY....WH...WHY DID YOU DO THAT?!"

"Do what," he asks?

"...DO YOU....WHAT WERE YOU....ARE YOU OUT OF YOUR...WHY DID YOU...DO THAT?!!?"

"I cleaned the table..."

"DAD!! WHY DID YOU PUSH ALL THE CRUMBS ONTO...THE...FLOOR?!"

"Thought I'd help out...don't worry. I'll sweep it up later..."

The women stood silenced in their kitchen. Their brains were finally and totally devoid of all thoughts and words. They looked at him and to each other and back to him and back to each other. My sister, who has been married to this man for nearly 35 years, threw up her hands and left the room. Their daughter continued to stand and literally stare, as if at an alien from Neptune, at her brilliant father for many remarkable moments and without words, for words did not come...And, the morale to this story is:

Men and women's brains work differently. We do things in completely different ways, and it still does not make sense to us. But men can quiet the bombarding thoughts of women and they can help around the house...sometimes....kind of. Amen.

The Contrived Romance

Since Americans take their lead from media, we can all probably agree that television and movies do present romance in over-kill. Perfectly groomed and gorgeous couples in their interior decorated homes, cooking perfectly ingenious meals with their perfectly dressed and mannered children; all the perfect flowers and kisses and thoughtful deeds and comments...I know, we women get a kick out of this kind of romance, but we also know that real thing comes once in 20 years and always with a whole lot of baggage. No, I'd venture to guess that romance is pretty over-blown and very, very contrived on TV. Women love contrived romance. It's the stuff poetry, mythology, and what romantic fantasies are made of, but real romance, like real life, is far different.

Modern, American romance tends to happen quickly. Meet, date, kiss, go to bed, and later, maybe get married or not. Maybe a man gives flowers to a lady on Valentine's Day and maybe a diamond ring. Maybe he gets down on one to knee to ask for her hand, or maybe they just move in together and co-habitat. Sometimes there are long courtships and engagements, and sometimes people marry after knowing each other for two weeks. But television and movie-style romance is very unusual in real life because real American people are imperfect, busy, impatient, easily bored, and likely broke. Unfortunately, women still desire and admire televised romance, and from the beginnings of her meaningful relationships, many women experience disappointments in the romance department.

First of all, Prince Charming is usually Prince Ordinary. He's average. He's not the wealthiest man, not the man of great intellect, nor the most romantic man. He is a human man with his peculiarities, strange habits, annoying hobbies, familial baggage, and obnoxious proclivities. He's every man.

And prince charming marries not the gorgeous and misunderstood maiden, but rather the average woman or girl. She's not Barbie. She's not physically perfect, and she's not a sex goddess. She's an ordinary female with her insecurities, her female fantasies about love, marriage, and her prince. And these days, she's also likely to be employed full-time, bossy, and self-centered, which also begins her adult, romantic dreams with her baggage in tow.

Brides and grooms spend time and money creating the fantasy wedding of the brides' inventions. The white gowns, the tuxedos, the flowers, the feasts, the honeymoons that begin marriages in debt and rather stupidly – but why not begin the marriage with contrivance, for more typically follows.

Marriage is very difficult to maintain in a selfish and materialistic culture. Marriages with children and/or stepchildren are even harder to maintain. Families with two working parents are simply gone from their homes too much to properly maintain houses and yards. And children in all America are now expected to play intramural or competitive sports, and ten other after-school activities or they are suspected of lacking resources and good parents. But the greatest difficulty for today's marriages has a great deal to do with the fantasy of marriage versus the reality of people. And both men and women are guilty of ill preparedness when it comes to living with someone "for life."

Youth is beauty, beauty youth – beautyouth. Look, I've invented a new word...When we marry and we are young, we like to look at each other because we are good looking. That's nice when combined with sex. Trouble is, we don't look the same in five years. We change. We all do. And very often, and particularly for men, this change disappoints. The post-pregnancy body of the woman disappoints. Sometimes, it repulses (Remember our places of truth – they are a must). The frequency of sex slows down with familiarity, time, life style, and lack of desire. Truth. The minute, and I mean the very minute a woman suspects that her husband is not sexually stimulated by her or her body, she's crushed to the core, insulted beyond insulting, and begins permanent behaviors born of insecurities, angers, suspicions, self-loathing, insane and yo-yo dieting, over-grooming, and manic house expectations that require perfections. The truth is that she is covering up her insecurities and angers with contrived decorations in her home and upon herself. I am absolutely convinced that the over-grooming and manic self-focusing, coupled with the bizarre trend to decorate homes as magazine photos, is born from the physical insecurities of women. I'll lay odds that I'm right. When women can't get themselves back to 16, and they hate their bodies and faces, I believe that they turn self-loathing into perfecting their homes, over-mastering husbands and children by becoming demanding, commanding, and neurotic, and by turning themselves into strangely painted, shaped, and colored dolls. I actually believe they subconsciously attempt to eliminate the real woman and create a new one. And I also believe they perform the artificial house and wife routine to try to keep their husbands. I hear feminists screaming now, but I'll still lay odds that I'm right on the money.

Now, with all this said and done, try to produce true romance in this house. Husbands or men feel very uncomfortable with cold, angry, and selfish women who live in sterilized, overly done houses. Husbands want homes where they are comfortable and needed. Women who are uncomfortable in their own skins, and who turn homes into galleries that cannot be disturbed, or can only be used for show and company, are emotionally unhealthy. Facts are facts.

True romance, which comes from love, desire, and passion, needs truth. Once again, the pesky truth. One can certainly have desire and passion without love, but without it, romance is unnecessary and uninspired. Therefore, it is my humble opinion that romance operates from truth. If the people are not true in body, mind, and spirit, real romance can't happen. And if women are plagued by physical self-hatreds, men will also focus upon her imperfections, as will children. I'm thinking that should one persist in self-loathing, others may jump on that bandwagon and help.

If you want a happy marriage, love yourselves. Love your homes. Love the people in them and focus there. Stop objectifying yourselves and your homes and create romance with truth, for if he loves the truth, you've found Prince Charming.

One suggestion came from a friend: If marriage licenses cost $10,000.00, maybe people would think very carefully about their partners, their futures, and their family planning goals. It's an interesting thought.

Reader's Request – Men at Home

Several readers asked for some words about men living with today's super-spending, self-deifying women. My first response is that I see men who are disenchanted, and I think that is a very bad sign. I've previously said that it frightens me that un-muse worthy women could ultimately be dangerous to the female gender. I truly believe that men need women. They may desire them sexually, but I think men function more civilly when engaged by women and engaged in families. Look at teenage boys who are without solid family bases – they roam in gangs and reek havoc in communities and upon teenage girls. Adult bachelor men are commonly disrespectful of women. Their conversations with other males about women are often exploitive. Their lifestyles are often sexually predatory. When men take their sex drives into marriages, they are fundamentally better for society as a whole. However, when they are married to women who deserve no respect and act like males, men tend to cease communicating, seethe beneath the surface, and their thoughts turn easily to other women or to packing up behaviors with other men.

Men who are trapped in the supporting roles of women who abuse their wages are angry. And women who grab the money and spend it foolishly on themselves treat men like objects called ATMs. Women need to remember that in American, men gather esteem from paychecks and are still defined by their ability to support families. When their money is washed down the drain, and there is nothing to show for their labors, men feels disrespected at the core – which is their maleness. Hence, castrating females – ones who are unkind and demanding, who think he's stupid, and who spend him into bankruptcy are commonly cheated on and eventually left. Sometimes men can get mean – really mean. Women should never make the mistake that men will only and ever simply verbalize anger. All men can blow.

Unhappy men avoid the family, children included, though it's not the children he resents. It's who he considers embarrassing – the bossy bitch with the bad attitude directed at him. They avoid these women at all costs. They turn her off with televisions, computers, jobs and physical labors. They avoid the demanding, sullen, crying, overly emotional, drunk, and insulting woman. As said before, men need intelligent women to run the home. If she can't, he is unsettled and slips into pack mode. In other words, he runs with the boys (football, basketball, baseball, TV, teams, bars, boys nights out, work, overtime, more work, helping his buddy build something, hunting, fishing, lying, and chasing women). All the things that drive women nuts—but he moves toward them and avoids the unhappy and artificial doghouse purposefully to get away from "her."

And the glamorous, bleached and tanned female? She ultimately gets the attention of the bachelors, but not the good men who want marriages and good mothers for their children. They don't get the men who want intelligent women who know how to build warm and safe homes and who are nurturers of children. They don't get men who need and cherish the skilled wife. No, those women get sexually driven men who want to be seen with perky breasted, young trophies. Good men aren't interested in lies for wives and for the mothers of their children.

But what if most women become physically artificially, non-mothering, angry spends thrifts? Well, number one, men will procreate elsewhere, and that's a given. Number two, their relationships with their children will die off because the tanned and bleached wife left behind will turn her children against him in her rages. Rages, you say? Oh, yes. Because when he leaves her, her lavish lifestyle will be over. She's not going to like that as so often it was his earnings that funded her day-spa treatments, wardrobe, her mini-mansion, her teeth and nails, and her $45,000.00 SUV. Yes, she's going to be really, really angry.

And finally, men disenchanted by incompetent, obnoxious, and over-spending women can be left with poorer opinions about women in general. This can lead to abusive behaviors toward future women and to gender enslavements in future generations. This may sound extreme, but it's not. There are plenty of current, living examples of contemporary men taking extraordinary powers over women and children through anger and force. It certainly deserves consideration because when one gender changes radically and for the worse, so does the other.

There is a balance to our interconnectedness. If we can simply find and acknowledge how it is that we work best together—two genders with innate skills to bring to the raising of children—and if we can use our skills intelligently and without contempt for one another, our children will grow reasonably and with respect for family. If the family becomes a miserable place for men, and if their needs as males cannot be met within the family, families will fail. The divorce rate, today, stands at 50-60%. What happens when the rate rises to 70% or 80%? How then will our culture or government deal with children of divorce? Women still don't earn as much as men in the workplace. Women should never forget these things. Caution is warranted. On top of all this, add males, as a gender, becoming thoroughly and in large numbers, fundamentally unhappy with their experiences with women, and potential outcomes can be horrible or even insane. We are vulnerable to each other in a thousand ways.

And one last thought, there is an old cliché or old wives tale, which goes something like this:

"The way to a man's heart is through his stomach."

I'll lay odds that this was the collective wisdom of a bunch of old wives because this is very true. As sexual attraction connects us, so does food prepared by women for men. Men love the idea that women cook for them. Yes, it originated with their mothers, but in the great scheme of humans on Earth, it originated with the first people and first families. Men hunted the food, women cooked food, and people ate the food together, which is probably how "families" originated – by sitting together around a fire and eating. I think "dinner" is probably one of the oldest, primordial traditions of human beings. And I'm quite sure that yummy food prepared by women was a turn-on way back when as it continues to be now. Women, known as wonderful cooks, are highly prized for their culinary skills by both husbands and children, alike – but for men, a fabulous meal prepared by a woman feels like a gift to him. Men, I've found, are very grateful for wonderful meals – truly grateful. When they are denied cooked food, I believe they are biologically unhappy. Though women tend to see food preparation and service as a female chore or servitude, males have been historically engaged in food gathering and preparation for their communities or tribes since the beginning of human time. They didn't hunt and fish for fun. Men played a critical part in the survival of tribes in their roles as hunter-gatherers. Food preparation is equally engrained in the primordial spirits of men. Western men don't have to hunt and fish for food anymore, but the old interests and connections still exist within them. Frankly, they would be far better off re-learning to hunt and fish, as the skills would help to solidify and redefine their maleness. Any woman who cooks food for her family is prized by her family. Don't mistake biology for slavery. Food preparation and mastery keeps men fascinated with women. If you don't cook for your families and if you often provide pizza or restaurant meals or drive-thru bags, you're doing yourself an enormous disservice because you are eliminating one of the oldest biological attractions that males have for females. In other words, if you don't cook for him, he'll feel unloved, unneeded, and will find someone who will. Simple enough.

It is terribly important that today's women understand that men's roles have become undefined in American culture. What has always given them definition as males is now up in the air. What is the purpose of the male gender when females can perform every one of his past functions minus one? Do we have a culture full of men who sense they are emasculated and somewhat useless? I don't know, but I would not like being in their shoes at this point in American history. The one function they are needed for – that of procreating and fatherhood – also seems to be in question. Now any woman can go to a sperm bank to become pregnant and marriage is not necessary. Divorce rates are astronomical, and many, many men simply avoid or even ditch their children due to child support arrearages and to avoid the mothers of their children. In a nutshell, men's roles have lessened in American culture as women's roles have enormously widened. The question is – are we in balance? I think the answer to that question is – we are not.

Do we take the freedoms away from American women that perhaps caused, at least in part, some of the imbalance? Absolutely not, but can we recreate the balance? Yes, we must. Everyone deserves to have purpose and definition, and if male and female parents are undefined within their households, children will flounder. We owe it to all future generations to acknowledge the roles of mothers and fathers and the unique skills they bring to families. Creating androgynous parents is anti-biology and anti-spiritual. We can't culturally abandon our natures by denying their importance in nature. Now is the time to be creative within our families, but also to be honest about the specific and individual needs of children, women, and men. We don't want to lay the groundwork for gender wars or disenchantments. If we do, it's all but historically guaranteed that women and children will suffer.

The Married American Woman

A friend called me the other day and said, "I think there is no need for marriage anymore." The woman who said this is a religious woman, and the comment certainly deserves consideration in this book.

I don't think many women like marriage anymore. My short, simplistic idea behind this thought is that marriage is hard work, and American women don't seem to care for hard work. It takes too much time away from grooming, decorating, and spending money. And many American women feel they are above hard work. Being seen as blue-collar, meaning doing work yourself, has become demeaning. Imagine that.

But women disengaged by today's marriages have larger and more complex issues than laziness. I believe many women are seething. They want something, but have everything. They need something, but can't define it. They are bored, but blame their boredoms on houses, husbands, and children. Still, it's more than this—more than standard, day-to-day, normal life. I wonder if American women feel compelled by their culture to dislike men. One wonders, if this were true, how we came to this point? Is it an old hatred? Is it a culturally imposed safety mechanism? Well, I have a few thoughts that I'm not settled with and fear opening the proverbial can of worms, but I'll put them on paper, risking my reputation as a non-conservative and non-liberal: I think perhaps we should look at political feminism and how it has affected American women.

I begin by saying that the suffragette movement in America was a blessing. It was desperately needed, and many women risked life and limb for its beginnings. But "feminism" was perhaps a tad inflicted upon us in the last 40+ years. I use the word "inflicted" because at some point in the last several decades, traditional roles for women became something less than professional and educated roles for women. The traditional roles of mother and housewife became somehow lessened as compared with women who became doctors, lawyers, and chiefs. Traditional women have even been maligned in feminist literature and attitudes as being trapped in service duties historically prescribed by males or as having copped out, so to speak. All I can say is – yes and no.

It is for certain that women had to break out of the house and role of housewife to evolve with their freedoms. Women had to become educated and employable to gain equal footing in the capitalist world of American men. They had to become employable with learned skills. But going from Point A to Point B did not require Point A to become embarrassing or less than Point B. As women spent their human history creating homes, which were meaningful to families and cultures, it is somehow very disrespectful to our ancestors to believe that the traditional roles of women are now pointless or less than professional women's roles today. Yet, many, many women seem to be very touchy about being viewed as housewife and mother. And I believe they take their sensitivity of traditional female chores and tasks out on men, or specifically, husbands. Equally, I think this is most clearly demonstrated by women's resentment of cooking and cleaning. Today's women want at least 50/50 sharing of household chores. And this makes sense if she is a professional, working women. However, and as I've said before, no one suits her. No one can perform house chores to her liking, and she blames others for her disappointment.

Also, today's women are resentful of cooking. Most do not know how to cook, which leave them feeling incompetent and embarrassed. But women also don't like the idea of being perceived by husbands and children as the family chef due to gender. This reeks of servitude, and women don't like to be perceived as servants to families. It's insulting because she is a free American woman who is no man's servant. Many women are even uncomfortable with taking the surnames of their husbands as, this too, might be perceived as too traditional and ownership-oriented. Well, it's certainly a quandary. I guess we must think that our mothers, grand mothers, and great-grand mothers were just pathetic victims of their culture....or were they? I can tell you this: In my family, most women have always been, until my generation, mothers and housewives. That was their definition. It's what they were. But at the same time, my mother, my grand mother, and my great-grand mother ruled the nest. Why? Because they were comfortable in their own skins and they knew who they were. They were not embarrassed by what they did for their livings. They had clear definition and they knew how to perform their jobs. Their husbands also had clear definition and knew how to perform their jobs. And between the two genders, they created homes and incomes that worked, and they were emotionally balanced and comfortable in marriage. Today, I see women who are honked off in the home. They have every luxury to make work easier, more pleasant, less physical, and quick to perform, yet women are angered by home's work. They seem to over-blow their workloads. They hate cooking meals, though they rarely cook meals. They are constantly at odds with their children who mess up houses, but they hire maids to clean and never teach their children how to clean. And for some reason, their homes are never cleaned well enough or to their satisfactions. So they seethe and take normal family needs and footprints as personal attacks on their gender.

In a way, it's very sad that there seems to be no good answer, no balance where women are accomplished within some kind of definition. If she is a housewife and mother, she's somehow copped-out of her potential. If she's a career woman, the culture worries about her children and so does she. If she tries to do both, the culture sees her as performing at about 50%. This is very sad.

I'm also hearing from many women that they actually prefer not to have sexual relations with their husbands. What I'm told is that they are too tired from work or they have to get up too early or that they simply don't want to deal with his physical needs. This is not a good sign. It's very, very anti-biological, but far beyond this, sex is needed to keep married people close. It's the easiest, cheapest, and most biological method in which to maintain closeness. For the female, who is the object of physical desire of the male, avoiding sex is breaking one of the most primary bonds that keep marriages together. The physical contact keeps the genders engaged and interested in one other. Sex helps to keep man and wife emotionally connected and close. But I'm hearing that many, many women are all but out of the marriage bed because they sense that sex is male domination and male need – but not theirs. This does not make sense. Though I can't believe I'm saying this, I know for a fact that my parents were making love into their mid-sixties. I know it for a fact because I walked in on them one fine day. And I'm hearing women in their 20's and 30's complaining about sex and, in some cases, all but refusing to participate, or I hear that "maybe once every month or two, and even "every year or two." Sorry, but this is not normal. And it seems to be always discussed in terms of a disrespecting disenchantment with husbands. This does not make sense.

I've seen younger women cringe at the touch of their husbands. I've seen them turn their faces away from impending kisses. I've seen women literally pull away from gentle and affectionate advances by husbands. And while her face is wincing, his falls with rejection that he clearly doesn't understand. Once again I say, have women not figured out that men need women – the key word being "need?"

Something is happening to the American marriage and I'm pretty sure that the changes are often coming from women. Sometimes I wonder if what happens to people who find themselves suddenly wealthy, and their often-ungraceful entrance into new wealth, is much akin to American women with their newer freedoms. Perhaps they are, in ways, unprepared to effectively operate with their freedom. I think of the poor kid who becomes a music legend overnight. Three months later, he lives in a $3,000,000.00 mansion, buys 30 cars, and is out dancing, drinking, and drugging in exclusive clubs every night of the week. Perhaps, too, many American women are emotionally unprepared to deal with new cultural realities and influences. The difference, of course, is that she is an adult though clearly and equally prone to cultural influence, and she's lived with her freedoms longer. But the kid living high on the hog is also, though for the short-term, happy. Many of today's women, it seems, are miserable at the core. And the only sense I can make of it is that when the innate biology and history of females changes – meaning that of mother, nest, and males – women are miserable because everything feels off. And again, I think intuitive consideration is in order. Women have got to figure out why they are so damned angry.

Another issue regarding the relevancy of marriage is, simply put, why should we? The real world of marriage claims to be of Holy union, but it is rarely lived that way. We don't have to marry to live together, and we can have children with or without, so why bother? The divorce rate is huge. The expense of legal divorce is astronomical. So why marry when you can live together and have children? Well, from a current cultural standpoint, I can't answer that question, but I do believe in promises. I believe in commitments and in family, and personally, I believe in God. Are families less than families outside of a marriage contract? Maybe not, but on the other hand, is it not better, somehow, to enter into love with a hope, or a promise, or an assumption that love lasts? If we could divorce our children, would we? I guess we have to ask ourselves what love means to us. Is it a really just a temporary virtue and should we consider it so? I don't know, but love, to me, is still larger than life. However, our familial failures in love tell us that we quit loving at least 50% of the time. I have no answers though the questions remain in the hearts and hopes of our children. Our souls are captured when we fall in love. And we continue to pray for the love of humanity. The questions remain the same.

What the World Sees

I just talked to a friend who recently took a Comparative Religions course at a university. I was told that currently, in India, the most frequently watched American television programs are 1) Baywatch and 2) World Wide Wrestling. My initial reaction was—thank God they aren't watching Desperate Housewives, Wife Swap, Nip Tuck, or The Swan. I cringe to think of the shows viewed by those who despise Americans. And I have to think, it's no wonder they believe we are sacrilegious and bad examples to the world, and I wonder why we ~~have~~ never understand that our remarkable freedoms bear responsibility? But how do we decide between gratuitous programming and programming with language, violence, nudity, and vice that also has meaning, social value, and educates? And who decides? Well, we don't want the radical right to decide or else we will all be watching reruns of Father Knows Best, Little House on the Prairie, and The Walton's every day and night. And if the decisions are left solely to the media executives, we'll get what we have now. I think we have, as viewers, to make clear to ourselves what is degrading, what is gratuitous, what is valueless, and what is culturally damaging because we are being overrun with gross, violent, and perverse entertainments—everywhere. And the biggest question – why do we stand by and watch while our culture is coarsened with what is obviously senseless garbage? All past cultures, which succumbed to widespread decadence, fell. Why do we accept or ignore vile entertainments, which are clearly offensive and amoral to most American people? Freedom of speech was never meant to be the freedom to contaminate goodness and innocence globally. And yes, I can hear all the arguments now – live and let live would be the best-condensed example. I agree, but mass communications were not created to corrupt and spread amoral messages or images (or were they?). And why has it become hayseed mentality to believe that goodness and innocence are wonderful? Why are people bullies or hawkish conservatives for wanting a wholesome country for their children? This has nothing to do with conservatism or liberalism. I happen to refuse both conservative and liberal political labels, but I still want my children safe and guarded from unethical and grotesque images. Don't you? Do you mind if your two, three, ten, and 13-year-olds watch graphic intercourse on TV? Do you mind if they see blown up, sliced up, or rotting corpses on television? Do you mind if they see beautiful, middle-class moms having sex with the pool man on television? Is that just fine with you? How I wish that our enemies were just watching Baywatch and the WWW! But the trouble is, they are watching what we watch, and they are judging our culture based upon what American television produces about American life. I'm going to take time out to look up the word "Infidel…" Be right back.

Okay—radical Muslims, the ones, we're told, who want us all dead, call Westerners "Infidels." Here's what Webster has to say:

Infidels—"…a disbeliever in the Divine origin."

Now I assume that an infidel to a Muslim person is one who does not believe in Muhammadism or Islam. If that's the case, then our Muslim enemies need to lighten up because we, as a country, were not founded upon Islamic tradition. And America's Christianity is an older religion and does, in fact, overlap with Islamic tradition via Abraham and the Old Testament. We should be able to get along, but when media globally propagates this slimy image of American people and culture, think of what the world sees. What must they think? I'm probably sounding like a Mid-Westerner about now, but most of us in this country are, in fact, Mid-Westerners and rooted in the Commandments of the Old Testament. Now, when television breaks every single Commandment and calls it entertainment, every single day and night on television, and in all other mass media outlets, we are uncomfortable. That doesn't make us fascist conservatives or religious fanatics. It makes us uncomfortable because our roots are old roots, and we believe that The Commandments are commandments and not requests. I might even suggest that Mid-Westerners are not left or right wing as a whole but very politically blended and balanced. We want all our Constitutional rights the same as anyone else, but we also want to maintain what we believe to be good. There's not a damned thing wrong with that.

What is also disconcerting is the image of American women on American television. I see the American female deteriorating yearly on TV. I see her portrayal as violent, crass, sexually exploitive and exploited, immodest, and again, plasticized with massive over-grooming (bleached teeth, false nails, overly made up, provocative clothing, unnatural hair, too thin, and publicly obnoxious in manner, voice, and tone). She is Hollywood – artificial—and very often portrayed as vamp, vixen, murdered female, adulteress, criminal, or brainless ignoramus—but she is almost always portrayed as a sex object in some way, shape, or form for entertainment purposes. I'm afraid that the world sees American women as stupid, shallow, sexy, grotesque, and available—even when they are mothers and wives. And I see men portrayed as violent, stupid, gullible, evil, strangely unfeeling, or dead via some blood bath. Why are we doing this and calling this entertainment? Religious peoples of any ilk are going to be horrified by American television. And furthermore, I do not believe that television is a reflection of most American people, whatsoever. So why do we allow this stuff to dominate day and night programming? Why are we watching? I think American people should agree to pick one or two days a week and refuse to turn on their sets for those days—a moratorium, so to speak—to protest the garbage that is forced upon the entire world by American TV. I think television has hurt us as individuals and globally, and yet I will be the first to admit that I watch television. It fascinates me. But there is just way too much heinous garbage on television, and we need, as a country, to take a stand against lowly programming.

The movie "Three Mile," based roughly on the life of Marshall Mathers, aka Eminem, is a riveting movie about a poor kid from Detroit who wants to become a rap star. The movie contained violence and serious language, but the movie had relevance, the language and violence a realistic portrayal of inner city life, and the movie had a message. It was a finely acted movie, and I loved it. I am not asking for censorship or prudish attitudes toward reality. And equally, I am not asking for Father Knows Best to run on prime time. I am asking that mindless gratuitous violence, meaningless degradations, and valueless and psyche-damaging visuals be challenged.

And many American women, many of whom I believe are bored to the point of instabilities, imitate televised images of wealthy women and Hollywood living. When the world sees American women as brainless, self-absorbed sluts on television, then television role models can and have been addictively dangerous. They are dangerous to us. We morally desensitize. Again I ask, what is wrong with wholesomeness? When did it go out of style? Why have drugs, alcohol, graphic sex of every persuasion, bloody violence, heinous crime, and vice become our primary sources of entertainment? This is what we enjoy? This is what we crave to see after our hard days working? This is how we relax and enjoy our evenings together with our families? Watching everything we believe to be gross and even sinful? When Americana-style living becomes hick-ish, fundamentalist, and country-bumpkin-ish, then something is terribly wrong. And once again I ask, is this media perpetration? Hmmm.

We must realize that desensitizing our spirits and the spirits of our children is cultural corruption, and the entire world is watching and judging. Maybe we should ask ourselves if there are at least some meaningful reasons for their disgust. I realize that all people in all cultures are equally susceptible to crude fascinations, but do we have to continue to support sick nonsense on TV and call it Freedom of Speech? I don't think so, and I know it is damaging our country's reputation all over the world. Could we please consider a one or two day-a-week moratorium to challenge corrupt media?

Media in America is way too powerful and totally out of control. It's trashing American women, in my opinion, and is a heinous influence on us and on our world neighbors. I don't even have to mention what American television does to children—we already know—but, at the same time, we've never done anything about it. It gets worse every year. One must wonder if ulterior motives are afoot...

We, as a people, need to make the media stop creating insidious programming, and the only way to force them away from televised crap is to refuse to watch. I think that media moratoriums need to be discussed in churches, wards, synagogues and temples, businesses and especially in homes, and I think that we, the people, need to insist that media stop producing valueless garbage for entertainment. Only when viewing numbers fall will they change direction. It is our viewing that continues to support the garbage. American people need to demonstrate to the world that we are not as media portrays us, and if we are, then God help us. It is clear that there is a mixed message about America that is making the world very nervous. Add to that our "enforced democracy," and then ask yourselves why we are globally despised.

Our government and all media belong to us. We pay for them, and we need to rein them in and lead them in a new direction. They now see themselves as all-powerful and global entities that can do what they want to do, when, in fact, they can only do what we allow them to do. This is our country, our culture, our hired politicians, our tax dollars, and our media, and they need a reality that is always and continuously checked—by us.

An Over-Punished and Repeating History

When we settled for Hollywood as "the" role model for female beauty, we settled for artifice and lies. When we settled for doctrine over faith, we settled for intellectual enslavements, corporate fiction, and lies. And when we settled for political entertainment over Constitutional rights, we settled for being fans and puppets and for more lies. It's an interesting position we find ourselves in—alive, functioning day to day, unsettled, and living lies that we know are lies. We have come to accept pretense on living scales.

Today I've been thinking about the historical phenomenon of the denial of women's opinions for thousands and thousands of years. And not just Westernized women, but globally and in most human cultures. I ask myself, could it be that this is the result of the Eve Syndrome—the original sinner? Is this why women's minds have been discounted for millennia?

Supposing the story of Adam and Eve has value, Eve broke one of God's two commandments, as there were only two at that time (make babies and don't eat the fruit). We are told there were ramifications for her mistake. But nowhere does the Bible say that women were to be forced into a human history that discounted their opinions, their thinking, and their minds. Imagine that, until the last 50 or 60 years, women's brainpower was discounted and shut off, purposefully, from most human ventures and throughout time. Why did males of nearly every culture commit this dastardly deed against women? Absolute control? Punishment? Ownership? Power? Does it not seem crazy that male humans simply refused to give females credit for anything? How could they, as a gender, have hated their female counterparts to this degree? Have they hated us, or was it something else that caused them to disallow women to participate in the needs of the tribe, the village, the city and town, the country, and the world? What happened to the world when half of its brainpower, throughout most of human history, was denied usage? It was.

If the story of Eve caused this punishment, then I believe she and we have paid for that crime. After all, Eve's sin was one sin against God. The Christian God has 10 Commandments people are supposed to follow. For Orthodox Jews, God mandates 613 Commandments, and as we all know, people throughout history have broken their commandments of faith, in every religion, billions of times. However, no sin was ever punished so severely as to shut off the brains, the choices, the intellectual capability, and the creativity of an entire gender for several millennia. The bizarre decision to refuse women the right to participate in the development of human cultures may have had results—do ya think?

Let's look at an easy example—one that American women can understand: traditional Muslim females. To this day, most Muslim women are not permitted to look at any man who is not her husband. She has to be covered, from head to toe, if out of the house. She may not speak to men who are outside of her family. She may not work. She may not drive. She may not go to school. And she may have her husband chosen for her when she is a child. She may not own anything. She may not worship God as she chooses. And if her marriage fails, and she lives through it, she may not have her children. How horrible, we believe. How terrible, we say. However, there is very little difference for any other women in history, in any culture, and throughout all time, except perhaps for the last 50 to 80 years and in the West. I say that the reason why the woman behind the burka bothers us so much is because she is the living example of women in history. She is the woman with no voice, no opinion, no respect, no power, and no meaning. And that, I believe, is the crux of the issue—women were denied meaning minus vaginas. And as hard as the Bible and other sacred texts have tried to explain roles for women, males refused to allow women with purpose or meaning. And today, I look at my contemporary American culture that is decaying the meaning women have certainly earned. This culture is corrupting those rights and meanings by defiling women on television and in Hollywood, day after day, night after night, 365 days a year. And each year, the degradations get worse and more insidious for the global public's viewing pleasure. I don't like the trend and I don't like what it's doing to the minds of American women and girls. Why is the degradation of women constant entertainment in America and in epidemic proportions? Why are women portrayed as stupid morons on commercials and porno sex objects on the billboards by American highways? Why are entire cities dedicated to sexualizing women for entertainment? Why are female children sexually harassed on school busses and in all schools every single day? Why are pre-pubescent girls the primary targets of pedophiles? Why are teenage girls the models for sexual beauty? And why are American women buying into the fashion, beauty, and medical entities efforts to "create" the perfect, sexual female? Why do mothers buy their female children bikini underwear and other sexually provocative clothing? And why are mothers slicing and dicing themselves, dieting for life, lifting and pealing their faces, bleaching their teeth, and turning themselves strange colors? It is because entities are marketing to them in insidious whispers that they are imperfect unless they are beautiful enough. This, to me, reeks of meaninglessness minus vagina. What do you make of it?

We live in a world that is still operated mostly by men. Historically, the world has fought wars and it continues to war with no end in sight while doctrines, laws, and rules are declared by men. It is at least interesting and food for thought that most women would choose not to war. Women want their children safe and biologically desire their children to survive. But that is assuming women operate as biological females. As Westernized women continue to degrade themselves by buying into marketing propagandas about themselves, their homes, and gender functions, they actually succumb to historical male thinking. They over-sexualize themselves and their daughters, and by doing so continue an old belief that women are incapable of and disinterested in intellect. Women continue the objectification of themselves as vaginas, and essentially remove their brains from the needs of community while focusing upon attraction and appearances.

As we are the luckiest women in all human history, I am personally repulsed every time I meet one more self-absorbed female. I am offended by her shallowness, which is a slap in the face to women who continue to suffer slaveries of every kind and extreme. If we do not wise up and realize that there is an undermining perpetrated upon us, we will never be respected, nor will we truly understand freedom. We can't continue to assist the cultural degradation of our gender and call it affluence and liberation. We are denying ourselves our brainpower and contributing nothing of value to our world. It seems we've learned history's lessons far too well.

Imagine, if you will, meeting one or two of the women in history who suffered and fought for your liberation. Imagine them escorting you to drop off your children in a daycare center and then to your spray-tanning spa. Then you take them with you to your hair appointment, your manicurist, and to your doctor to discuss your many problems. Then you will take them to lunch at your favorite bistro. They will escort you to shop for new mirrors and new decorations for one of your bathrooms. And then they can observe your afternoon nap while your maid cleans your large and perfect house. They can observe your landscapers at work while you retrieve your children from the daycare center at 5:30 in the afternoon. And then, they can watch your anger elevate at the prospect of making dinner, dealing with your husband, and your children's evening homework and baths. They can observe the anger caused by the clothing that needs laundered when all you want to do is watch evening television with a glass of wine. They will observe the relationship between you and your husband, which is non-communicative and sullen. And they will observe your children who live their lives unhappily while walking on eggshells that they pray will not litter your house and further elevate your anger. Imagine, for one minute, how your mothers in freedom would feel about your treatment of freedom. Think about it.

Pretty Bullies

Back in the old days, "bullies" were boys. They pounded on the weak, verbally tormented the awkward, and insulted fat kids. They hunted for victims in packs in their schools and neighborhoods. They were feared and avoided at all costs by their victims, and they were typically ten-years-old. And most grew up to be decent people.

Today, girls are bullies, too, and their numbers in schools have been growing for decades. They also tend to run in packs that we call social clicks and tend to be of two types: gangs or cheerleaders. Gang girls are scary. They are typically urban kids from poor neighborhoods and they are very, very tough. They fight, knife, steal, and defend their territories with their male counterparts. They are fierce female warriors and criminals.

Mothers and schools create cheerleader gangs. They are educated in the arts of shunning, self-elevation, and taught they are role models for other girls. They are verbally cutting, cruel, mocking, and they deliberately insult and gossip to cause social damage to their victims.

They are the cream of the crop of teenage beauty in American schools, and they usually date school athletes. They are also party girls, often sexually active, and typically the children of the middle and upper-middle classes.

All female gangs are dangerous. They cause irreparable damage to girls who do not fit in or are not accepted by the groups. Urban girl gangs are often from broken or unmade homes and often do not attend school. They are usually street kids who spend their days fighting for survival, money, and drugs with their gang partners. They are kids who are victims of culture, poverty, and who lack compassion, parents, and mentorship.

Cheerleaders are created, educated, and primarily invented by mothers, and this deserves our attention for they are also feared and avoided by many in schools. Cheerleaders are the creation of angry women. Are all cheerleaders awful? No. But talk to any girls about the cheerleaders in any

American school, and you will hear the same comments and stories about the prettiest girls on campus. The number one comment is, "They're mean."

Cheerleading camps are usually orchestrated, led, and taught by former cheerleading moms. The girls are taught how to dance, bounce, smile; how to style their hair, what color lipstick to wear, and they are required to stay together as a social group. They are instructed on attire, behavior, diet, and avoiding friends who do not elevate their social status. They are warned about associations with "the bad kids" in schools. But the most interesting track for cheerleaders-in-training demonstrates how they are role models for other girls. In fact, they are trained to believe they are better than other girls due to physical beauty and social status, and that girls, who are less beautiful or poorer, are unfit for friendship and to be avoided at all costs. Cheerleading is a breeding ground for class segregation and the mean, critical, and judgmental female. As I have said before in this book, we have to begin in places of truth.

I have found over the years that mothers are becoming brutal toward children. They are bossy to a point of dictatorship. Just last week, I heard a mother say to a child, "...That's an order! Not a request!" When the child challenged the order, the mother literally fisted up, leaned far into the child's personal space, and intimidated the child with her body and clenched fists. I saw the child literally back up and run. I've seen and heard the same scenario on soccer fields. Mothers have become far more unwilling to even hear the points of view of children. They expect immediate attention, silence, and adherence to orders from children – even those who are not their own. One wonders if this kind of treatment of children does not indicate feelings of powerlessness in women, and a need to assert power over something.

I've heard women bark orders loudly and in public to children. Not requests, but absolute orders where no compromise, no consideration, no options, and no responses are permitted, whatsoever. It's the type of language and expression you'd expect to hear in military boot camps or prisons, but not toward children. I've seen women slap children on their heads and backs while barking orders. I've seen women screaming at children for sitting down, standing up, drinking water, for day dreaming, for turning cart wheels, and for resting after tremendous physical activity during soccer—literally screaming threats and commands and in front of anyone. I see women punishing children for being children. And I see an unreasonable anger that is actually not anger at all, but rage that manifests from an irrational desire to control something. And these women are also orchestrating the social training grounds for girls—cheerleading, for instance. This is scary stuff. And I continue my concern that American women are literally on an edge of stability themselves when innate mothering instincts are not functioning normally. I see women who are losing it publicly, and in large numbers, when it comes to their reactions to children. They become unglued with rage at the slightest infraction of a child's behavior or when children question their fury. And I also see women trying to regain composure and calm themselves after their explosions of temper. I see women attempting to "shake it off," which is a masculine behavior and response to anger. I see women who don't even attempt false kindness. These women are actively involved with the social and emotional destruction of their daughters' psyches. Not only do they sexualize their female children with clothing like short-shorts with giant words printed on the seats, belly pants and shirts, which are clearly sexually exploitive, but they also model criticism, explosive and dictatorial temperaments, and expectations of physical perfections. In other words, they model unbalanced behavior. So sorry, but true.

Today's cheerleader will be tomorrow's mother. She will see herself as prettier than most, socially elevated above most; she will be critical of most, she will be self-absorbed and looks-oriented, she will be demanding of her way as a superior person, and she will be hell on her children, for she will expect them to be beautiful, obedient, and perfect. And I fear that today's mothers are today's mental cases as they attempt to recreate their youth and beauty, ever so angrily, in their daughters. Hence, the next subject of this book, which addresses an American mental illness called "beauty."

The Mental Illness of Beauty

This is the section of the self-inflicted wound. American women bought into the corporately imposed "perfect female" hook, line, and sinker. Here she is:

- Under weight with large, fake breasts and a flawless face
- Teen aged
- Tall and willowy
- Long, flowing hair
- Provocative in revealing clothing
- Heavily made up with cosmetics
- Sexually stimulating to men

Her name is Barbie. Her name is model. Her name is cheerleader. She is 16, virginal or innocent looking, flawless and/or airbrushed. She is unmarried and pre-motherhood. She is a sexy girly-girl. And she is the apex of American beauty.

She was created by the fashion, make-up, porno, educational, and media industries. She is a movie star, a young whore, a music star, a cheerleader, and virginal. In other words, she doesn't exist unless she is in high school or junior high school. All boys want her and all men desire her. She is a trophy and a sexual fantasy. The problem with her is that the moment she is no longer all of these things, all desirability leaves her. Her physical beauty fades. She looses her edge and her confidence.

College destroys her because she is no longer innocently dumb. She develops intellect. Sex, engagement, or marriage destroys her because she looses virginal fascination. Motherhood destroys her because her body becomes touched with experience and pregnancy. Aging from teen to womanhood removes her youthful, sexual power over men. But worst of all, these said experiences of today's American female create self-loathing as teenage beauty has become her role model for female perfection. She looses, coming or going, by virtue of coming of age and growing into full female potential. American females hate themselves as women, which is why they are so vested in the physical appearances of their daughters. It is why they will go to every expense to be beautiful. It is why they hate their bodies. It is why they support, through their self-loathing, all industries that create the concepts of perfect women. And no women on the planet can win. They just keep spending money in hopes that something will get them back to 16.

Today's women are physically and mentally contrived. They are obsessive and compulsive about their bodies, their hair, their faces, and their clothing. They wake up feeling old, ugly, fat, frustrated, and angry because they are not young enough. They are obsessed with their bodies, the food they put into their bodies, and they hate themselves for every dessert, every fried food, every hamburger and carbohydrate they consume. So they work out, diet, starve, loose weight, gain weight, diet, starve, and work out. They hate themselves for eating. And they continue the cycles for decades. This is not normal behavior. It is obsessive, compulsive, destructive, addictive, disordered, and self-loathing behavior. And it's all based upon a culturally imposed model of beauty. The mental illness has nothing to do with husbands or boyfriends, self-improvement, or health. It has to do with how the culture has defined beauty. And we bought it, and continue to buy it with billions and billions of dollars each and every year, and nothing works.

American women, in insane numbers, are involved in the daily destruction of their psyches, spirits, bank accounts, free time, happiness, focused parenting, marriages, homemaking, and health due to their abject obsession with their looks. Nothing works, but they continue, year after year, to search for 16. Instead they find self-loathing, anger, jealousies of every make and measure, and self-mutilations of every kind. No pain is too great. No amount of money is too great to spend. No amount of neglect to children and home matters. Women want beauty but they can never get enough and it's never good enough. They are never, ever beautiful enough. And because of this, they are never, ever, good enough women. This, my friends, is mental illness. You can minimize it any way you want. You can make all the health and social excuses you want to make, but the bottom line is the line of truth: In America, if you are not a young and beautiful enough female, you are simply not good enough, period.

But, this is also a self-inflicted mania that mimics, to a tee, full-blown addictive and abnormal reasoning. Women cannot be teenagers. And it infects our daughters like the illness it is—self-loathing, self-obsession, and narcissism. We are simply lost in an obsession with ourselves and can't seem to veer off obsession's tracks. It is psychopathic self-involvement based in anger and self-destruction. The obsession with youthful beauty steals time and attention from children and husbands, robs women of maturity, robs joy and confidence, and models pure and diagnosable narcissism. And worst of all, it deadens the intellect.

When you bought into the hype, and you certainly have, you demeaned freedom by believing that your faces and bodies were of planetary importance. Do you really think that your bleached teeth, tanned skins, lifted or pealed faces; your manicures, fake breasts, lipo'd butt, or your hair matter to your children, husbands, or community? Do you think that, after you've spent hours at the day spas, your family notices the make-up applied by the cosmetologist, the professionally tweezed eyebrows, and the wax job – or do they notice that dinner is crap, if it exists at all? Or do they notice your anger, which never seems to diminish or be resolved? Do they notice your obsession with what is or is not in the refrigerator, your diets, your workouts, and your constant complaining about your body and face? And are your daughters following down your paths of self-loathing?

Beauty has become a mental illness and multi-millions of American women are sick with its symptoms. You need to get help and make peace with your bodies. You need to accept aging and find its unique beauty. If you can't, you need to get help. And you need to stop believing that you are so damned important that a day without your physical perfection means the destruction of joy on Earth. Truthfully ladies, maybe your pathological self-involvement does, in fact, rob joy from many, many others. And, guaranteed, your self-obsession is a boring drag. It is, however, culturally understandable.

Ugly Truth

The worst thing that a human being can be is an ugly female. American women know this. Ugly women are not women – they are its. They deserve no conversation, no love, no invitations, no dates, no concerns, no thoughtfulness, no help, no anything. They actually don't exist because no one wants to be around them. They are hideous and you wouldn't want to be seen with one. You are screwed if you are born an ugly female. And you are especially repulsive if you are an ugly woman in America. You just might as well move.

Eleanor Roosevelt, Whoopi Goldberg, Kirstie Alley, Delta Burke, Oprah Winfrey, Condoleeza Rice, just to name a few – these women have had more attacks than the Mid-East. Why? Because they were not ideal, not pretty enough, and not perfect. It matters not what they did or do—they don't look right—and America has sliced them to personal pieces, ridiculing them in public for their faces and weights. Every tabloid and every insult globally distributed and given to the whole world—it's interesting how women are up for public, and even global scrutiny when it comes to their bodies and faces. It's a trend that begins in schools and continues for the rest of their lives. And women's magazines, in particular, jumped like frogs onto this bandwagon. There may be as many as 500 magazines devoted to the weights and faces of women and how to make them better. And, of course, it's women who buy them in their desperations to look better.

Your author is a heavy woman, and it never ceases to amaze me how people feel totally free to comment on my weight, which is my body. They feel absolutely within their rights to tell me what I should do to and with my body, and they feel compelled to tell me they do not like the look of my body. All think they have the magic pill or diet or workout routine or surgeon, but many make public conversation with the topic of my body. I would be prettier, healthier, feel better, look better, on and on and on, and never, ever, has it dawned on any one, ever, that their taking liberty with the topic of my body is perhaps, shall we say, a personal invasion of the privacy of my body (and rude, insensitive, and presumptuously poorly mannered). Every time someone decides to throw up the topic of my body for conversation, I sit thinking, "...how dare you...". It's a physical invasion and an absolute demand that I hear I am not good enough. It is no wonder American women are a mess when the public is compelled to criticize them at the very core, which is their gender, and to pretend the criticism is kindness. Telling a woman she is fat or ugly causes emotional damage to women. And yet, people who are over-weight or homely can't get through a day without public insult. As I've said before, the persecution begins in elementary school and continues for the rest of their lives, and it demonstrates the cultural acceptance of punishing imperfect women.

"You should have by-pass surgery."
"You should go on Atkins."
"You should get your nose fixed."
"You should wear black."
"You should get your teeth fixed."
"You need a dye job."
"You need a pedicure."
"You should talk to a plastic surgeon."

This is the endless list and largest list in human history, and women write and rewrite it.

Homely women simply give up as children because they are convinced of their unworthiness as children. And though the initial criticisms of their faces and bodies typically come from male children, life-long and unending criticisms come from women and the women's beauty industries. And the message? It doesn't matter who you are or what you do or contribute – you are ugly and that matters first and far more. Until we get this problem solved, we are objects, first and foremost.

The primary fallout of a culture obsessed with looks is emotional damage that is gender-sized. Women become compulsive about how they look to the point of mutilations, eating disorders, and addictions, which is one more terrible truth to face.

Women and Their Substances

Anyone my age knows about drugs, alcohol, and addictions. We were all introduced to them in schools and were experts by late teenage-hood. Some of us used them, some of us used them and didn't make it, and some of us escaped their draw, but we were very familiar with the substances that were sold in our schools, stores, and in our neighborhoods.

Now substances are even more available as there is simply so much more to choose from via the black market, the pharmaceutical industries, the prime time TV ads, and restaurants that all serve liquor. We sense that people with addictions make the international world of governments and big cartels go around. And it was only a matter of time before the "health" industries would also discover that addictions were profitable. Man, oh man, there are a lot of drugs out there now – a whole lot to choose from – and especially when a culture prefers you to be addicted to perfection. So again, we, as women, have another topic to consider, and that is the pharmaceutical industry that we support with our addictions to "health" and "beauty."

Let's begin with vitamins. Women love vitamins. There are commercials about women's vitamins and supplements on television every single day. Bone health, menopause health, skin health, stress health, iron health, pre-natal health, teeth, nail, and hair health—all marketed to women. I guess all those females from previous centuries in time must have been sickly wrecks. Sure, we live longer, but we don't die frequently during childbirth anymore. It's just amazing to me how many supplements are marketed to women – kind of another suggestion that we need help with our goal of perfection.

Then, of course, there are the drugs to help us deal with our depressions. Zoloft, Paxil, Wellbutrin, Celebrex, and Cerefin are also marketed in happy commercials on our TV sets every single day and, specifically, to women. Now, add to these diet drugs—the untested and unapproved diet and energy supplements, which are also marketed on television. Zantrex, Metabolife,

Stackers, Phen-Fen, Celebrex for weight loss, Xenical, Merida, Diet Fuel, Ripped Fuel, on and on and on – and once again, it is women, not men, who support the health and beauty drug markets.

Then we can add the diuretics and laxatives that de-bloat women and shave off a few pounds and, of course, the diets themselves. And the lotions and potions for our skins and the hair serums and the cosmetics and polishes—when, ladies, does it stop? At what point does our addiction to appearance become completely and dangerously moronic? There is really no wonder that we take anti-depressants, is there? We have become the most vulnerable and gullible fools on the planet and big industry knows it. We make multi-millionaires of laboratory rats who come up with worthless and dangerous concoctions to sell to us. There is nothing we won't put into or onto our bodies for the sake of beauty. There is nothing we won't try and no potential harms great enough to curb our desire for youth and beauty, and yet we have continued, for decades, to call this "health." Maybe what women need are anti-psychotic drugs since we are nuts for self-destruction.

I personally know women who take the following on a daily basis:

Advil or Motrin
Metabolife
Xenical
Between five to 10 vitamins and supplements
Zoloft or Wellbutrin
Ex-Lax
Diet Fuel
Calcium and Vitamin D
Insulin
Potassium
Hypertension meds

...just to name a few. On top of the fact that many American women are addicted to legal drugs, they also see therapists and starve themselves with one or more diets, and they are addicted to running and working out. This is not an overstatement, but rather the normal state of female affairs in this country. Women are addicted to drugs of all kinds and in epidemic numbers. Now, add to that the elite usage of cocaine and liquor and wine and tobacco, and what you have are brain and physical deaths waiting to happen. And American women call this "health." Now ask yourselves about your self-worth and how you are viewed by American culture and its health industry.

You are an addict with money, and you are physically and emotionally unhealthy. How does that truth feel? Are you inventing, as I speak, the reasons why I am wrong? I'd venture to say that you don't need one 12-step program but five or six if not hospitalized intervention. I'd also venture to say that if you stopped all your drugs, diets, and workout routines that you would be sick for a while, which is called withdrawal. Well, here's one more thing to think about, and think you should because your beauty drugs are most likely in your medicine cabinets just waiting for your daughters, and your dieting, workout, and angry perfections and compulsions are right around the corners from your children. Don't be surprised when they also become addicts, because, as we know, addictions run in families. Enough said, but will it be heard or denied?

The Career

Half of the American workforce is female. Women generate half of all household incomes. The process of pitting men and women in roles of competition for jobs didn't begin well. It was a rough road for both genders, but as the costs of houses and automobiles rose, so did the mandate of the two-income family. My first house was purchased in 1974 for $21.000.00 dollars. I live in the same size and kind house today that I lived in then, a three bedroom, one½ bath ranch. The house I live in today would sell for around $150,000.00. My point is made. The two-income family is required by most people just to pay the mortgage and drive to work.

But there were social and personal consequences to the widespread employment of women. The obvious and first issue was children and childcare. The next issue was women had money and therefore power and opinions that were finally to be heard and considered. The other change that occurred was how genders would view and treat each other at the workplaces while they were competing for jobs, promotions, and authority. In time, many of the initial difficulties ironed themselves out, and men and women became comfortable with duel employment and financial responsibilities. But perhaps a few subconscious issues have continued to plague us in the workplace. Perhaps the workplace does, in fact, lessen some of the biological fascinations between man and women. For instance, does muse ever bump heads with competition? Does chivalry become less inspired with authority figures in pumps? Does competing for best provider roles change our perceptions of each other as males and females? Of course – yes—to all the above. Males are no longer providers. Parents are providers. And this has been an extremely difficult social and emotional transition for males. It lessened their historical and familial definitions as the masculine gender. Women earning wages took something defining away from men. And the transition for women has also been a double-edged sword. It gave them freedom, education, and resources, but it also damaged their children, their children's educations, and it created a living environment where women were literally burning the candle at both ends, because the home work did not stop and was not shared by men, as a rule. With all women have gained as employed people, they have also absorbed tremendous feelings of guilt and anger.

In essence, employed men and women changed on very core and internal levels. Problems continue, and there are no good answers as we live in a two-income and Federal Reserve/debt-based culture. Our roles have merged and now we expect the equal sharing of all work. I suggest we at least consider that the merger did damage our attractions to each other in ways. Perhaps it is a tad more difficult to romanticize each other when we perceive ourselves as interchangeable as well as the competition. Don't get me wrong. I'm not suggesting that women quit careers to be solely mothers and housewives. Neither am I suggesting that men should be sole providers. Those days are long gone and they had their faults, too, and particularly to women. But the changes mandate thought and consideration for children did, in fact, lose mothers to employment, and it changed their lives.

The mass education and employment of women built the childcare industry to its current and deplorable condition. It institutionalized infants, pre-schoolers, and after-schoolers. Parents gave up power over their children and their educations when both parents opted for or were forced into careers. And the result? The American family drastically changed. Men and women and their views toward and expectations of each other drastically changed. And the lives of children went downhill. Some may disagree, but they would be wrong. Children have suffered from being separated from their mothers for the last 40 years. Most children in daycare centers have been too hungry, too tired, too wound up, too ignored, too un-held and unloved during most of their days, and they have had 10 to 12 hour days of separation imposed upon them by the two-income culture. This has never been ideal or even a halfway decent option for children, and they suffer in ways that most parents insist upon ignoring. And I get the feeling that many parents blame each other for the guilt they both feel but refuse to or won't act upon.

As a culture, we have failed our children. We thought we could build cute, colorful buildings to take them to and compensate. We thought we could hire women and pay them minimum wage to love, care for, and teach our children. We thought we could open these buildings at 6:00 a.m. and leave our children in them for 12 hours, five days a week, and be good parents. Denial. Denial. Denial.

We thought we could pay strangers to be parents to our children – to potty train them, to teach them to walk and read, to teach them to be creative and to have good manners. Denial. Instead, our children, beginning from infancy, developed insecurities and behaviors, which parents didn't like. And the children took their sullen insecurities and behaviors home, at night, when they were too tired, too hungry, too anxious from separation, and shocked their parents with angers, resentments, obnoxious behaviors, and depressions. Truth hurts, doesn't it?

Men and women, husbands and wives, then blame each other for their disruptive and unhappy children, and their expectations that one parent or the other will handle the evening work at home. It's really quite a mess and I don't see anyone or any entity even attempting to come up with solutions that are based upon the well being of children. Instead, more and more daycare centers are built keeping longer and longer hours of operation so that moms and dads can compete in the workplace. It is for certain your children are going to be horrible parents, for they haven't been nurtured. You can't buy nurturing. You can't buy mother's love and care when you purposefully avoid it 12 hours a day for income and careers. Consider, if you will, that American children are now routinely in "school" from infancy through the age of 17 or 18 – and then on to college for four to six+ years. You think social re-engineering "entities" haven't jumped on that opportunity?

The answers are only to be found with creativity, bravery, by eliminating lavish life styles, and putting the needs of your children above your own – and that includes money and promotion. Think it over. I know there are no easy answers when culture and government gives you no encouragement or support, but the bottom line is clear: your children or yourselves—what's it going to be?

It is also to be considered that "centers and schools" are mandating very specific educational tracks for your children, and those tracks are also working to emotionally remove your children from you and your belief systems. This we also know and, strangely, ignore.

The Nutshell – The Cultural Devastation of American Women

I once read an article on a website that considered the historical powers of very wealthy men. And I pondered the amassing of power by men, and the historical results of males corrupted by power. It has been the downfall of so much, and has caused the brutal death of so many. And it seems to be one of the greatest errors of the human species and never seriously addressed. So much brutality and crime could have been avoided if mankind could or would have addressed the issue of the over-empowerment of men. And as the aforementioned article suggested, a handful of them now determine the fate of all human life on this planet while drinking in a hotel. Strange days.

This brought me to thinking about women who, as a gender, have had a difficult time—historically speaking. Sure, there have been a few female leaders in history, but the bulk of female experience has been unhappy in many ways. Until the 20th Century, the pleasantness of a woman's life depended upon the decency and kindness of her husband. If she was given to a good man, she was lucky. If she was given to a cruel man, it didn't matter. And this is true for most women of all cultures, for most women throughout history were not given the right to choose husbands until very recent history. Many, many women still do not have that right.

The 20th Century did, indeed, help some of the female gender. Mostly, it allowed for some opinions to be heard, and in many countries, for votes to be cast. This was a long time coming, and was certainly warranted as women had given birth, cleaned, cooked, planted, and toiled for these rights for centuries. However, many Westernized women took a wrong turn, and particularly so in the United States. American women allowed for the corruption of feminism – the complete and total corruption of feminism – and the results have devastated our nation.

Feminism was not born in the Suffragette Movement. The Suffragettes were women who fought, and mostly with dignity, for the right to vote and higher education. They were not culture-damaging women. They were mothers and wives. They fought for representation and fairness and nothing more. Feminism, as defined by today's standards, was born during the Sexual Revolution, which was born from widespread recreational drug use by American teenagers. Why no one ever made the connection is beyond me, but that is the truth of the matter. When youths in high schools and colleges were high, widespread sexual activity was the fallout. It's the same phenomenon as the "bar" mentality – get drunk and sleep with anybody who is willing. Once American youth were openly sleeping with all their friends, including ones of the same sex, and at the same time under the influence of a one or two decade-long marijuana, cocaine, LSD, hashish, amphetamine party, a mindset kicked in, which perverted the very essence of feminism.

The resulting politicizing of feminism all but destroyed what it means to be a natural and biological female. In fact, feminism became a movement based upon anger, demands, and a demand that women think and believe in a prescribed and documented agenda. Political feminism actually worked to recapture the free will of women. Try disagreeing with a political feminist and discover what a dumb ass your free will has become. Try disagreeing with anything a political feminist has to say about anything. You would get the same attitude and look from a radical environmentalist – no compromise, no reflection, no regard or respect for the opinion of another, no deals. They are unapproachable, arrogant, and believe themselves to be intellectual elites – much akin to their CFR/Bilderberg brothers.

Feminism is not brute-force politics. With bated breath, I will tell you what feminism is. Feminism is the result of women who feed and grow their spiritual and biological gifts. That is its sole definition. There is not one American woman who needs a political feminist to define her, represent her, craft her opinions, or her needs as a woman.

Women have the ability to become spiritually advanced creatures, above and beyond the ability of most men to do so. The instinctual and intuitive abilities of women, if nurtured, if paid attention to, and if understood, carry significant mental and intellectual power. Women have a higher link, for lack of a better term, to spiritual sensation.

The easiest way to demonstrate this link is in their ability to develop a mental and loving relationship with children in utero. Most women love their children before they are seen, before they are born. Women have the ability to comprehend and to know the unknown, much like faith, and if this ability is nurtured and developed, it can carry forth with great accuracy into the world.

Women sense danger. Women sense problems. Women sense safety. Women sense future needs. These are vital skills and they are biological gifts, but they are also gifts that evolve around motherhood, children, and nest. So sorry, but truth is not a political agenda. Women who become what contemporary culture refers to as "psychic" are simply women who develop their instincts and intuitions.

Women who are working 70 hours a week, spending time in board meetings knocking out deals, running to gyms, hair, and nail salons, and shopping while their children are in daycare centers 10 to 12 hours a day are simply incapable of real feminism. Feminism happens when you develop your female strengths. High-powered careers, gyms, hair and nail salons, and shopping while the kids are sorrow-filled in daycare all work to create anger and resentments in women. Truth hurts, doesn't it? Most self-inflected wounds do.

Political feminism has taken motherhood, nest, the womanly arts of cooking, gardening, and nurturing away from women. Political feminism has also helped to mandate the two-income family by insisting that American women work outside of the home or be looked down upon by contemporary culture. Political feminism helped to build the deplorable daycare industry, which is literally filled with minimum wage female employees – thanks a lot. Political feminism helped to build the illegal immigrant nanny and handyman industry – thanks a lot. And political feminism helped to build the drive-through junk food industry since working women don't want to cook, and therefore, don't know how to cook – thanks a lot. Political feminism helped to build and grow the mental health/big pharma industry, which now specifically targets women and children as in New Freedom Initiative on Mental Health. Thanks one hell of a lot. AND political feminism helped to destroy, literally destroy, the public education system in the United States of America, which is now a full-blown dictatorship. How dare you, and how dare you claim to represent freedom for women.

Many, many contemporary American women are emotional messes. They are pathologically vain, materialistic as clearly demonstrated in their overly decorated, sterile homes, and landscaped yards; are grossly self-involved, horrible and mean-spirited mothers and wives, and they are constantly, incessantly, angry and neurotic. American women are shallow. They openly accept television, Hollywood, and magazines as role models for their daughters and themselves. They abuse money and spend thousands upon thousands of dollars annually for beauty regimens, diet supplements, day spas, trinkets, and gym memberships. Many are addicted to a whole array of over-the-counter drugs and beauty aids. This is liberation?

American women wouldn't understand feminism or liberation if it smacked them in the head. They are so far removed from their spiritual and biological natures that mirrors have become their solace and definition. And the results? Take a look at the condition of American children, marriages, and home lives, and then ask what role political feminism has played to make American women a global laughing stock while their children die spiritual and emotional deaths. American women are so off track they don't even realize that 90% of televised commercials and programming are insulting, objectifying, or making light of their gender. Then add the death of the Constitution to this heap, which political feminism has been instrumentally shredding for decades and voila! Liberation and freedom of all kinds—gone – poof – just like that!

Can we at least agree that too much power corrupts men, which is historically provable and factual? Can we at least agree that American women have been absurdly vulnerable to cultural BS? We are all in want of truth, and our children suffer deplorably due to its lacking. We must try to restore as many foundations for our children as we can, but we have to begin with ourselves and go from there. If we don't or won't recognize basic, and I mean the really basic and core truths, complex CFR/political-style lies, and those of their feminist sisters, rule the day.

I mean, seriously—you want to purposefully destroy a perfectly good culture? Give dictatorial powers to a small group of rich men and destroy the female psyche. Then sit back and watch that culture go up in flames.

Part III – Self-Definition

Altering the Universe of a Child

People have paired up since the beginnings of human history. We know males, females, and their children created tribes, and those tribes created communities, towns, cities, and nationalities. We know when two genders create children, the whole pattern, from tribe to nationality, repeats again and again.

We don't recall in our collective souls why this pattern began. Many believe it was ordained by Heaven. Many believe that the protection of infants was at the core of the familial pattern. Others believe that sex drive alone gave birth to family living. I've even heard it said that the physical domination of females by males created the father-mother-child scenario with mothers as original captives or slaves. It's all interesting and food for thought, but I, myself, don't buy any of the above in full.

No matter what you believe, the social structure of family stuck to all cultures, globally, like glue. I believe the creation of the family structure is far more likely to have developed from protectionism and the building of armies. The more men that stuck together to hunt for food and to fight off predatory animals and other tribes, the greater the food supply and potential for new women. I believe that the raising of the first primordial armies laid the groundwork for the evolution of the mom-dad-child structure, which the world continues to live by to this day. It is a comfortable structure. It creates children, armies, jobs, satisfies needs, puts bison, berries, and nuts on the table, and serves to create family dynasties of all social levels. The structure creates cultural glue.

Throughout history, there have been thousands of alternative lifestyles. They are usually invented and performed by young adults, and the alternatives usually evolve into traditional lifestyles with age and the coming of children. And that's fine. Everyone has the right to question the world's waters and its institutions. That is the most important function of youth. They keep traditions on their toes, and if traditions become stupid or out of date, young people will find them out and change them. This may be the purest function of young people and their critical eyes. But....

Divorce devastates most children. It doesn't bother them for a day or a week or a month. It damages their spirits, which means they are permanently changed. For lack of a better explanation, let's just say this: When you change the oldest traditions of humankind, the one's that go back to the very beginnings of humankind, you tamper with the wiring of the psyches, instincts, and natures of human beings. Perhaps a child's need for male and female protectors is simply universal law for all children. Perhaps they grow up feeling better, more secure, and with different or more brain synapses when raised by a male and a female who are biologically related to them. And perhaps any interference with parenthood is anti-nature for children. Perhaps I'm a fuddy-duddy and don't know what I'm talking about. Perhaps the damage to my children is not visible and obvious after 30 years. Perhaps not, indeed...

When you consider the child-parent relationship in universal versus culture-specific terms, none of the cultural excuses for bad parenting work. You simply consider children who are born totally vulnerable to people and nature, and you identify their needs from ages newborn through late teenage-hood. Read the last sentence again and think about it. You are determining the basic needs of children ages newborn through teenage-hood. This does not include computers, ipods, cable TV, bicycles, electric scooters, stereo's, home theaters, designer sneakers and jeans, malls, maids, junk food, automobiles, extracurricular sports, on and on and on...

Focus on life needs: Food, clothing, shelter, and attention. Now, ask yourselves if one person can faithfully and successfully provide these things over the course of 17 to 20 years. The answer, of course, is no...not on a daily basis over two decades. You can't serve the hour-by-hour needs of a child if you are ill, injured, hospitalized, or working full-time or working two jobs. Now, the single mothers in today's world (multi-millions of them), who have raised children alone, will argue this point. In fact, I argue for I have taken sole care of children 20 times while sick with flues and bronchitis. I have driven myself, with children in tow, to the hospital after falling and breaking my ankle. As I've said before, you'd be very surprised to know the real lives of single mothers, and you would be very sorry for your treatment of them. But still and ideally, two parents are better than one – for all involved. And children somehow grow up more secure in who they are and with more understanding of themselves and their places in the world with male and female role models. It just seems to work better for kids to have two parents. So the loss of a parent to divorce is spirit-changing and damaging. There, it's out in the open and we said it! Much as molestation and physical abuse of children is spirit changing, so is divorce. Divorce leaves permanent scars on people. Painful thought...isn't it, but important to believe. Perhaps there really are changes that universally devastate children. Americans really need to think about this for if and when you decide to divorce your spouse, you forever change the spirit of your child(ren). One more time: *You forever change the spirit of your child.*

The Big Stretch

This section is entitled "The Big Stretch" as I make leaps into theories that may or may not be reasonable. As I've said, I am no expert on human beings much less genders, but neither is anyone else. When culture and social norms change on a daily basis, no one can really guess how people will react or be affected in longer terms. So I will offer questions more than answers and food for thought more than assurances. This is the chapter of guessing.

We'll begin with the simple premise that females are females due to children who grow inside their bodies. That's simple. But what else causes female-ness? Smaller than males, less musculature, less bone density, higher voices, less fur, breasts, an extra rib – that's all I can think of at the moment. So here we have a simplistic definition of the biological female.

What is a cultural female? Well, as of today, I'd say she was liberated in most ways, educated, looks and career-oriented. I really can't think of other definitions of an American cultural female. But this doesn't feel right because I believe I almost described a male in today's America. Perhaps this is good. Perhaps making cultural identity androgynous demonstrates the leveling of power in our culture's playing field. Maybe so, but I am not comfortable with the blending. I want females in America to retain their gender-specific uniqueness and skills. Are we actually losing gender purpose in contemporary American culture? Is biology unuseful in contemporary culture? As males and females, are we virtually indistinguishable when it comes to the continuance of culture? Are we interchangeable? Does culture not need genders to survive?

The obvious answer is, yes. We need to procreate to ensure the survival of our species. That takes two tangoing genders, but it also does not answer the question, which is: Can culture—the ways of living, working, functioning, believing, and getting by on a daily basis – can culture operate, minus procreation, without genders? It's an interesting question. I suppose that the short answer to that question is yes. But, to me, that's science fiction.

This moment, as I type, I am looking out a window at a Sugar Maple in full color, and a soaking rain falling straight down, and it is very dark outside, though it is 10:15 a.m. It is October 18th and the birthday of my youngest grandchild. My youngest daughter is at the zoo this morning, and I know she is wet and cold.

I am caring for four children today: two six-month-old babies, a five-year-old Kindergartener, and a six-year-old First Grader, who I will see this afternoon. Both the babies are sleeping, and my five-year-old boy is curled up next to wood stove while watching a Tweetie Bird cartoon. In 30 minutes I will begin lunch and make noon bottles. And I realize how traditionally gender-defined my life has become. Everything about my job and days is now biologically female-driven. I cook, clean, and care for children. That is the job I created for myself in order to stay home with my last child. It was my choice and one that I never regretted. My immediate world, however, had a big problem with this decision. My mother thought home daycare was a huge mistake as I was "wasting a master's degree!" My sister, for years, thought daycare was a saving grace as she thought I couldn't find a job. And over the years, many soccer parents thought I was an uneducated hillbilly eecking out a living. They could have known better, but they rarely, if ever, talked to me or asked me any questions. Yes, I have become the most traditionally based female I know, and it amazes me to this day.

But as to the question of culture and gender, perhaps I simply went in the wrong direction. Perhaps females are gender-defined in American culture. Maybe the American female, as defined by or in her culture, is:

- Shallow
- Vain
- Selfish
- Spoiled
- Lazy
- Demanding
- Judgmental
- Snobbish
- Rude
- Crass

- Non-maternal
- Materialistic
- Very uncomfortable in natural skin
- A spend thrift
- Obsessive-compulsive
- Passive-aggressive
- A tad (or more) pathological

In America, everything is possible – from the most heinous to God's grace—it's all here. But traditions die fast in this county – really fast. In 50 years, women have lost the entire fabric and function of their roles as females since they've been on the planet. That's fast. I feel very lucky to have been the exact, right age to witness both the traditional and non-traditional female. It's a truly unique and pivotal window in human history. And the ultimate question is – where do we go from here? Back to traditions, forward to redefinition, or do we stay the course becoming the first artificial living robot on the planet.

Today I will tell you that I'm opting for redefinition. As I've said before, we simply cannot go back. Morphing into Barbie Dolls should be SCI-FI channel material and not grooming – the whole beauty concept having become completely grotesque, weird, and self-mutilating. So redefinition seems to be the only possibility though, honestly, that feels strange, too. But redefine—we must—because our children and grandchildren are standing on the vertex of our crossroads. Whatever direction we choose, they will follow and become.

While we look at the possible outcomes of our decisions, let's grow our daughters and have them become the outcomes vs. ourselves. Children have a way of demonstrating things simply. With that said, let's begin with American Female as Barbie. Now just add your daughter's name in the blank, and off we'll go:

Scenario Number One

____________ wakes up in the morning and packs her gym bag, her microwave lunch, and dresses for work. She gets the kids up and pulls them into their clothes and is angry by 6:30 a.m. because they are not waking up and cooperating. She turns on the TV and tells them to sit down and watch while she makes up her face. She re-emerges at 7:10 and tells the kids to get into the car. On the way, she calls her husband on the cell phone and says he'll have to pick up the kids because she's going to the gym after work and to tan. She is terse and impolite to her husband. She arrives at daycare with tired, hungry kids, walks them in and leaves immediately. She goes to work for nine hours, leaves work, goes to the gym, exercises and tans, and leaves the gym, but stops for one drink with a gym friend before going home. When she arrives, the kids have had Mac Donald's, her husband is angered by her late arrival, and she is tired and doesn't care. And, oh by the way, she also stopped by a super-store before going home and charged $250.00 on the Visa for new workout attire, new sneakers, a gold bracelet, two new skillets and two new decorating mirrors. She arrives home at 9:00 p.m. It was her night out because she has to take the kids to a soccer game tomorrow, and the next night she has a hair appointment, and her husband can just deal with it! This is a typical as it gets in today's world.

Scenario Number Two

______________ gets up in the morning and gets her kids out of bed, dressed, and turns the television on and tells them to watch while she gets ready for work. Out the door at 6:45 a.m., she drops them off at daycare at 7:00 a.m. She goes to the office where she has a 7:30 a.m. breakfast meeting and then an 8:30 meeting. At 9:30, the baby-sitter calls and tells her that one of her children is sick. She begs the sitter to allow the child to stay until she can finish her client presentation and her noon lunch meeting with her development staff. She calls the sitter at 2:15 p.m., and says she will try to have her husband pick up the children early and that she will call her back. At 3:00, she calls the sitter again and says that her husband is on the road and cannot retrieve the children, and that she will leave at 3:30 p.m. At 3:50, she calls the sitter and says she is on her way. She arrives at 4:30 p.m., to retrieve her sick child and her other children. She is rattled, breathy, guilty as sin, and a career women with responsibilities that cannot be ignored. She is soooo sorry. She has pizza and pop in the car. This is at least a once a week scenario for daycare providers.

Scenario Number Three

_____________ gets a lot of work done between 6:30 a.m. and 9:00 a.m., which is when her children usually get out of bed. She tells her children,

"Good morning!" and makes them breakfast. When her children are eating their oatmeal, fruit, and milk, she turns on their cartoons, and she returns to her computer and works for another hour. At 11:15 p.m., she gets the kids dressed to go outside and play. She takes her laptop and sits on the porch and watches and enjoys her children and their noises while she continues her work. She calls her boss to report in and to discuss work issues, and then she goes inside to begin lunch. She then calls the children in to read a book and sets up the paint set at the kitchen table and lets them paint while she works on lunch. At 12:45 p.m., ___________ and her children eat together and talk and laugh. At 1:30, the children lie down for naps and ___________ continues her work until 3:15 p.m., when the children get up from their naps. Then __________ and the kids go to the grocery store, the library, and the post office. They return home and the kids have a snack while _____________ starts dinner at 4:40 p.m. Her husband comes in at 5:15, and they kiss. They have a quick dinner because they all have to get to the soccer field for the four-year-old's game at 6:00. They all get home from the game at 7:20. __________ and her husband helps with the kids' bathes, and bedtime stories. Lights out at 8:30 p.m. And life is pretty darned good. ___________ has one ½-day meeting a week with her company and boss, and on that day, dad works it out with his employer to also work from home. This is the rare scenario, but it is the happiest chance for children. It is the one that takes determination, creativity, and commitment. In 13 years of daycare, I've seen it once.

The question is, which scenario would you choose for your daughter and grand children—Woman as Barbie, Woman as Professional Job Addict, or Woman as Working Mother at Home with Her Children? Impossible or not, maybe jobs should come second to children's needs, and that making money should demand that one or both parents earn livings from their homes. I pulled it off. Is it a perfect world for my child and me? No. But I'm home, each and every day, and she is secure and raised, fed, and cared for my her mother. Do I miss the world of adults? Sometimes, but I've also found that I have time for my interests, which I simply would not have unless I worked from home. Do I feel like I've wasted my education? No. 90% of my university education was wasted, social blue printing money. Do I feel like a domestic? Yes, and surprisingly, I like the label very much. I've become a better cook, better organized, and somehow, I know who I am, where, in the professional world, I never knew who I was or where I was going. I honestly didn't know what my professional goals were or if I had any. I simply use to get up, go to work, and come home mentally tired and do another full-time job. That's what I remember most.

So what does it all mean for 21st Century women in America – worker bees, career women, mothers, wives, and free? I don't know except that we do bare enormous responsibility. More than, say, for the women of 100, 200, or 1,000 years ago? I don't think so. After all, they were growing and harvesting and cooking and preserving the food; they were shearing the sheep, spinning the wool, weaving the fabric, and making the clothes. They were cutting the trees, making the huts and houses, and fetching the water. And they were pregnant constantly. Were their lives easier than ours? Nope. Like I've said before, we've lost our edge. And we are very angry much of the time, but I don't know what we're angry about…I can't figure it out – except for this: maybe American culture doesn't know what it's doing. Maybe it's simply speeding down a very fast track – but to where, and who's driving? Maybe transnational global business is driving or some other economic entity, but where is it taking us? It's scary because it's frazzling not only how we live but also who we are at the very core of our identities, which is first and foremost, female or male.

I have no answers or even near to complete guesses, but we need to search for them because our children need definition. I knew who my parents were. My children know who I am, but will yours? How will they define the term "mother?" What will "home" mean to them or will it simply be another semi-permanent building to temporarily occupy like a work, daycare, or school building? And will it have any more meaning for them than an employment office or a dictatorial classroom? Will it be the nest where they grew to know their parents and develop identities and traditions? Is the nest unnecessary? Have humans evolved into utilitarian beings over and above family members? We must think this through and decide if the furious pace of our culture is taking us down a path of choice or a path of enforced and utilitarian momentum. Perhaps the greatest entitlement of human beings is the right to self-determination. Do you still have that right?

You Can't Take a Stand Without a Backbone

Knowing the suffering powerlessness of women over the millennia, I also know that they have been the bravest human beings on Earth. Braver than men fighting wars? Oh, yes, because women faced their enslavements with children in tow. They faced every violence, degradation, disrespect, and poverty while caring for their children and many up to the moments of their death. Never would I doubt that women have been the bravest of the brave and the strongest of the strong. But I certainly do worry that we are not capable of such bravery and strength today. We've dummied up. We've lost our edge, and our souls know it. Fortitude has turned to boredom and nonsensical tasks like over-shopping and over-decorating. Inner strength has turned into dull angers that are always just beneath the surface. And we feel it. So how do we pull out of the clutches of a shallow and self-absorbed culture? I'll tell you how. We group together, like we always have, and we think it through. We plan and organize and we go to work, just like women always have. One woman helps another and another, and we get jobs done with our children beside us. But how do we begin? For me, when I need to regroup, think, and make a plan, I edit down the contents of my house and I clean. And somehow, perspective is gained through an empty closet or drawer. I know you know what I mean. And then, I call or email friends, my sister, or others and discuss my concerns, fears, or feelings, and between us, sense is made. That's just how simple it all actually is. Women are born planners and organizers. Now, we just need to get on board the reality train and do what needs to be done versus what advertisers and marketers want us to do (which means "spend"). Let us promise to once and for all stop the tanning beds for God's sake. And let us promise to store some food, water, money, and medical supplies each and every week. Let us promise to never again bleach our teeth and to apply our own make-up. Just with these few things, you can buy $1,000.00 worth of things your family really needs or you can begin your savings for emergencies. Then, I ask you to gather your friends and to investigate, together, food storage. Contact a LDS friend or neighbor, or call a LDS church, which is called a Ward, and ask if there would be a woman in your area who would be willing to show you her pantry so that you can see the value for yourselves of putting back for a rainy day. And I ask you to cook at least one meal a day for your children and then work toward two meals each day.

It takes backbone to admit to stupidities. I still smoke cigarettes and I struggle spiritually, so I know about stupid behaviors, and I know how hard it is to strengthen my back. As I said, I am ordinary and with plenty of failings, but I'm worried and scared for my country. I know that we are losing freedoms and going downhill, and we don't have a chance without the strength, intuition and biological intelligence of women. If we don't regain our gifts, our children's futures are at risk, and I believe that with all my heart. The United States of American cannot survive without the real and true brilliance of women.

What Is Woman's Intuition?

Auh! The $50,000,000.00 question! Some think intuition is akin to an old wives tale. Some don't believe in intuition. Some think it's a magical power that women possess. Some, in the past, have called it witchcraft. Some think it's God's gift to women. Me? I don't know where it came from. I only know that it exists and I know that I get my strongest intuitions around or resulting from my children and grandchildren. For me, intuition is connected to motherhood and to nature. Intuition is a sensing of something. It's a feeling that actions need to be taken or avoided. It's a warning, at times, and a call to action at other times. But I know it exists and works, and I am sure that all women have the ability to strengthen its workings.

I believe we developed intuitive natures by virtue of the fact that children develop in our bodies. We learned awareness on the internal level by being capable of falling in love with our children in utero and by developing skills to communicate with them in utero. We know our children when they are born in the way, I believe, that God knows us. It is a profound and undefined knowing, and it is the core of womanhood. As our children grow outside of our bodies, the undefined knowing grows, as in we know when they are unwell. We know when they are hungry. We know when they are afraid without the telling. We sense problems around our children. We just know. Look at cat, dog, or bird mothers. They know what to do the second litters are born. They are untaught. They just know. It is the same biology, the same profundity, and it is as old as time. Female intuition is complex for it does go beyond our children and into the world at large. Some call it psychic power. Some call it prophecy. But what I know is that intuition is fundamental truth. Women sense trouble. They sense danger, and they sense need. Nature can also spur intuitive intelligence. Gardening grows intuitive thoughts. Forests do, as well. Water, perhaps above all nature's marvels, kick-starts intuitive sensations or feelings. And intuition breeds perspective. And what a blessing that is – living in a time and culture where perspective is virtually lost on human beings who believe themselves to be the greatest living intelligence. Intuition reconnects women to nature, their spiritual potential, and their biological knowledge. Intuition rattles women internally and moves and clears a path to their connections to God. Intuition is a built-in safety net and warning system for women and their children. Without it, women are vulnerable to the thousand insanities of cultures. Without it, we wouldn't be here because we would have lost our minds thousands of years ago. Intuition is our foundation of freedom and peace of mind. It saved the female gender from its profound historical sadness. It taught us to be intelligent and to wait and to silence ourselves when necessary. It taught us to be mothers. It taught us to cook and to care about nutrition. It taught us to make homes warm and pleasant and to love and care for men. And it taught us to evolve and to spread our intelligence as soon as we were able. And now, intuition tells me that it is time for women to come back to the wisdoms and skills that modern culture has vehemently disrespected and robbed. I would never ask women to go back to the enslavements of the past. I would never ask a woman to be a stay-at-home mom or to quit her career. We are needed in the world of business and government and finance, but we must reestablish our natures as women and the powers that fuel those natures. We cannot continue to blow off our children in a world that wants to blow. We have to come back to the home and re-create it. We have to build our homes with safeguards and fundamental necessities. There can be no more generations of American children who are quickly and silently going insane with neglect, boredom, lack of nutrition, lethargy, and indoctrination in the schools. Listen your intuition. It will tell you what you need to do.

Where Does Life Without Intuition Lead?

As both spiritual and worldly creatures, we know what is wrong in our world and with ourselves. We live on a planet of opposites. God gave the world in order that choices could be made through experience. We live and interact with horrible things around us every day. We are constantly faced with decision-making that tests our ethics, spirituality, and morality. Should I drink alcohol? Should I smoke cigarettes? Should I take a vacation? Should I take this job? Should I cook this meal? Should I buy this nail polish? Should I buy this car? Should I claim this deduction? Should I take in this stray animal? Should I read this book? Should I allow my children to be educated by a government with a social-political mission? Should I try to talk to my jerk-face neighbor?

We live in a world of dilemmas and opposites, and we have the tools to deal with our world. But all people, from all parts of the globe, know that things are changing in ways that have never before been known. People are feeling insecure, unsure, and globally nervous. And we know for certain that frightened people are terribly, terribly dangerous. Unfortunately, this is particularly true for men. Unsettled men, as history clearly demonstrates, are wild and violent. Men, who function with clearly defined purpose and routines—wife, children, home, jobs, and with definition, are civilized. Men without are not. This is the human history of males.

Today, and globally, a very large and growing number of young males are being led to insane courses of action. These men are poor, without hope, without personal purpose, and vulnerable. No one considers "terrorists" as vulnerable, but that is what they are, and they are wild and violent. If they continue on missions to reek havoc and destruction, then other men will also become vulnerable to fear and anger, and they too will become just as wild and violent. The result of this kind of nightmare will be beyond what human beings can fathom, because with men, as we all know, competitions demand clear winners, and their weapons are now weapons of mass destruction. This competition will be the ultimate brutality. I believe the whole world knows this and is terrified and getting angrier.

What we all face turns into political pressure on television. It's how we are appeased, calmed, and manipulated, but "terrorism" is not politics. Women know this. Men can call it anything they want. They can call it Islam versus Christianity and Judaism, Zionism versus Gentiles, East versus West, Oil versus American consumption, poverty versus affluence, western armies versus radical Islamic terrorists, globalist-corporate governance versus the masses of humanity—but women know that this war is only man against man in what they believe to be a manipulated, and perhaps, final battle. They will use any excuse and every justification to wage any kind of war. Their stories can change a thousand times in the course of a year, and on both sides, but they will prove to the world each other's sinful and beastly agendas. It's the same war that has always been fought, but it may be the last time for all men.

So here we are – 21st Century American women. Hell is breaking loose and that is not a cliché. Weapon systems, armies, tactics, reconnaissance, satellites, global positioning systems, unmanned aircraft, verichips, national ID cards, manufactured super viruses, nuclear bunker bombs, fingerprint and iris ID technology, governmentally-imposed educational curriculums, North Korea, Iran, Iraq, Israel, Palestine, Russia, Malaysia, Nigeria, Sudan, Venezuela, Philippines, Spain, tens of millions who have died of Aids in Africa, and again, armies and weapon systems of mass destruction amassing in every corner on Earth. And American women, in large numbers, are decorating, tanning, bleaching their teeth, buying jewelry and spending every dime they have. Never, in all of history, was the timing so off for the complete breakdown of common sense in women. Never was the need for their instincts and intuitions so important and necessary. However, if we, as women, continue on our road to self-omnipotence, what will our county look like in the next decade? What will our families become? Who will our children mimic and what lessons will they have learned? What will parenthood mean to them and your grandchildren? Aside from nuclear or pandemic annihilation, here is what I think is possible:

- America becomes a Third-World country and our living standards comply. Our country is bankrupt, and upwards of 90% of American people live far beyond their means and are in chronic and governmentally orchestrated debt due to the Federal Reserve System.
- We are losing more and more control of our children to the government, its schools, and to a culture and judicial system that disrespects and mistreats our children every day of the year.
- We are at the doorstep of losing our overly expensive mortgaged homes when interest rates are raised and raised over the next decade.
- As China and Japan are now America's creditors, and who, today, have gathered our debt to the tune of 70+% of our Gross Nation Product, and as the value of the American dollar continues to strategically decline, it is only a matter of months – probably less than one year, before repayment to our Asia creditors will be instigated.
- The draft is inevitable and will be reinstated within years. This time it will include female children as per current and pending legislation.
- The full-time employment of women will skyrocket within the next one to two years. Most American women and senior citizens will be working outside of the home.
- Senior citizens will sell or lose their homes in droves and their social security will be cut in half before it permanently ends.
- Medical insurance will become completely unaffordable and most Americans will be uninsured.
- All our current standards of living will drop ten-fold.
- Gasoline and drinking water will be rationed within the next one to five years, and the cost will skyrocket.
- Due to the competition for food and the demands of Chinese and Indian populations, the cost of food will skyrocket within two to five years.
- Families and marriages will disintegrate due to debt, blame, and hatreds between men and women.
- Children will, in droves, become little more than wards of the "regions" as most women work full-time jobs.
- Children will be raised according to the desires of the states, the federal government, schools, and their employment agendas.
- Fathers will disappear in mass numbers to military service and divorce.
- Children will be poor and little more than state-sponsored orphans.

That is what my intelligence, my intuition, and my instincts tell me. The days of America's debt-based affluence are over. And I believe that we are already actively engaged in global WWIII, though no one will admit to the fact that global economics is based upon the constant creation and maintenance of war.

And I worry, profoundly, for America's children. How can we explain this to them? How did the world get to this point? Perhaps it's because we, as American people, ignored our leadership while living stupidly and selfishly on the highest of credit card hogs. Perhaps it's because the world's poor are insane with helplessness, geo-political religion, and hatred. Who knows? But as women, with children, we are needed. I'm sure as rain that our nurturing instincts will be required on a large scale. I'm sure that our ability to cook and grow food will be a saving grace some day. And I believe, with all my heart, that there will come a time when our intuitions can and will save many.

I am glad and grateful to have been born a free, American woman in the 20th Century. I am one of the luckiest women in the history of the human race, and so are you. It is time for our gratitude to demonstrate itself in deeds and works. It is time for women to participate in the most important time perhaps in human history because, frankly, we have been a huge part of the problem. A country's female gender can't collapse without dreadful fallout. If in doubt, check the conditions of Iraq, Saudi Arabia, or Talaban Afghanistan where the male gender and its good senses collapsed. We must take hold of our true gifts and powers and prepare, prepare, prepare our families and ourselves. This country and its children cannot survive without the strength, wisdom, and intuition of its women. History proved this.

Does Going Forward Mean Going Back?

As utopian as it may seem, returning to the old ways of living and romanticizing the old days is not an option. Once science discovers new inventions, new weapons, and new ways of living, there's no going back. You can't undo scientific discoveries no matter how hard you try or disapprove of them. Science, like time, marches on. And science, just like people, has given the best and worst of itself to people and their greed.

It must seem that I hope for a return to more agricultural living and simpler times. Maybe I do, but I'm no fool in thinking that women will ever again, in most of the Western world, give up anything to anyone. That's a good thing, and I know it. But I can and do hope for reflection, on a very large scale, of Westernized women and, particularly, of American women. I fear their self-loathing. I fear their guilt. I fear the tendency to meld their gender with the male gender by becoming akin to men in their senses of duty and the expectation that others will nurture and care for their children so that they can make their dents in the world. I'm afraid of those dents. And I'm afraid of the dents and gashes of their children. Should women go to college and work in the professional world? Absolutely, yes. Should they be leaders of industry, politics, and professional role models for young women? It's a must. But can women remain women and equally give to their children and homes. They haven't—and they must, for failing the family, which means children and husbands, means that others or other institutions will pick up the slack and make the decisions. The institution of marriage itself is already in question and in the legislature and courtrooms of America, as is public education and childcare. Why? Because the traditional role of women as primary care takers and educators of children is over. The question is—what can we do, as women, to recreate the strong, united family and function with common sense in a changed and very dangerous world? How do we pull it off? We begin by editing. And the first thing that has to go is the pathological vanity. No more tanning, false nails, bleached teeth, professionally applied make-up, massages, wax jobs, facials, laser resurfacings, pedicures and manicures (unless you're over the age of 60), professional trainers, and therapy sessions (unless you're mentally ill and diagnosed). If you must use a beautician, get your hair trimmed from time to time, but cancel the weekly or daily dependency. Anyone, including a five-year-old, can wash and dry hair.

Next, keep one credit card empty – meaning unused, for emergencies. Get a debit card for your checking account and have one, and only one, credit card. Cut up all the rest and PAY THEM OFF. Do not charge vacations. Pay for them in cash, which also means, save for vacations that are well earned.

Get rid of half the stuff in your houses. Clear them out. Sell any and all furniture that children can't use or touch. It's insulting that you bought this furniture to begin with and disrespectful to your children. Get rid of it, and buy furniture FOR the family – sturdy, comfortable furniture. And never, ever again be so stupid as to buy white carpeting. Children, no matter how careful, cannot win with white carpeting. You do not take carpeting directions from realtors. You buy carpeting based on the number and ages of your children. It seems retarded to me that this would actually need to be said.

Next, get rid of your expensive new automobiles and buy sensible cars that are one or two years old. Don't ever go into stupid debt with automobiles. The Dodge does exactly same thing as the Lexus and the giant SUV – from point A to point B—and if your social status and ego is based upon the price, model, bells, and whistles of the car you drive, see a therapist.

Clear out all your closets, drawers, and cabinets. It is a fact that getting rid of things you don't need readies you for personal and internal changes. I don't know why it works, but it does.

After you make these edits in your life, make a four-season list of things the family needs to do together. For instance, in the Fall, clean out the garage and buy yourselves some shelving for storing food and supplies. Put your vegetable and flowerbeds to bed for the winter. Buy four to 10 cords of firewood and clean the chimney. Get your Halloween decorations ready, get out your winter tools, rake your leaves and clean your gutters. Do it as a family. Each season has its chores and children need to learn them. They won't learn them from your laborers. They need to learn from you so that they learn the knowledge, the skills, and realize the importance. If home's work is not important to you, it will never be important to them.

Next, learn the art of storing food and supplies. Here, you can pick up some wisdom of the past and, by doing so, you will be teaching your children common sense, prudence, thinking ahead, and preparing for a rainy day. You must teach children to be sensible in actions and deeds. You cannot talk or bully a child to sensibility. You must demonstrate it and explain it by living it.

Now, let's talk about childcare, which is a fact and a must in America. When a middle-class person or couple has no choice but to buy a house for $100,000.00 (a very little, inexpensive house), then 90% of the time, two people are going to have to work to support it and the people who live in it. Therefore, find the best caretaker you can for your child, and when your workday is over, retrieve your child at the same time every day. And do not leave your children in daycare while you go out to self-serve and spend money. Take them with you. They deserve your time and your wanting them to be with you. They want to be with you – not me. Equally, consider very carefully the decision to purchase a house. Eminent Domain is real. So is the political intention of taking all privately owned property.

Rainy Days Could Be Much More than Wet

I have a Mormon friend and neighbor. She prefers to be called a Latter Day Saint or LDS. Her name is Jennifer and she has a six children. Jennifer taught me about the LDS tradition of storing food, and I have to tell you this story.

I met Jennifer at a soccer meeting. She had five kids in tow then—one being a newborn. That's pretty much all I remember. After that meeting, I just remember we were friends. So, one day, I stopped by her house for one reason or another, and her garage door was opened. In that garage was a veritable grocery store of shelving full of food. I'd guess a thousand cans of what people with kids eat – peanut butter, jelly, green beans, corn, spaghetti o's, baking staples, beans, on and on, and just literally more food in one house than I'd ever seen. I thought she was absolutely nuts. So I went home and thought about her "pantry" and it just drove me crazy. I thought about it and thought about it. So the next time I went to her house, I asked her if I could just walk through her garage and look at her food. "Oh, please do!" she said, and so I again toured the garage and took serious mental notes.

"Why," I asked her?

"Well, if Rick (her husband) died, I would be in very bad shape with all these children if I didn't have my food storage." That made sense. I understood that, and I knew that Rick traveled frequently on airplanes and overseas. So, I went home and, again, her food storage haunted me. I couldn't stop thinking about her garage, and I also could not stop thinking about my vulnerable condition as a single parent, self-employed, and what, on God's green Earth, would I do if I got sick or hurt with one or two week's worth of groceries in the house. Well, I caught the food storage bug. I made initial investments in shelving, water barrels, wheat, rice, oatmeal, powdered milk, beans, baking staples and cooking oils. Then I started buying canned goods in bulk. Three years later, I have six month to one year's supply of pantry storage in my garage. Sound extreme? Believe me, I understand, but you are wrong. Now let's talk about being busy women.

At the beginning of this book, I said that we are all constantly busy because we are supposed to be. That is what adults, who are responsible for children, are – they're busy. And none of us have enough money because we spend like crazy idiots on stupid and unneeded things. It's an American cultural problem (which we are all going to pay for dearly and soon). Buying in bulk and storing food will save families at least $2,000.00 annually. You will never run out and there will never be a day that you "have to" go to the store if you store properly. Food storage and preparedness conjures up images of paranoid people in backwoods Idaho with guns and anti-government sentiments. That, my American sisters, would be a big mistake in thinking. Food and supplies stored for your family in case of problems are not wacko notions. Storing food and supplies, in fact, are about the oldest notions you can have. In fact, some call these notions "instincts." My mother had a large pantry when I was a child. She kept it because she lived through the depression and because her mother had a pantry. Mom's pantry was an unused stairwell, and it was floor to ceiling food. My Grandmother's pantry was on her porch, in a closet in her kitchen, and in every bathroom cupboard. I remember she had hundreds and hundreds of rolls of toilet paper. And my Great-Grandmother kept a pantry of canned items from her garden. I know this from my mother who worked in her gardens as a child and helped her to can the harvest. Food storage is what people used to call "preparing for a rainy day." They kept back food, water, medical supplies, soaps, money, and sewing supplies and fabrics. Hmmm. Sounds…intelligent. Sounds like responsible adults using their thinking caps. But today, in America, the home of spendthrifts and gadget addicts, food storage has become peculiar …something those Latter Day Saints do. Well, I hate to burst your judgmental bubbles, but if you are not storing food and water and medical supplies and clothing and money, you are going to be in for a rough time. And here, I offer to you the greatest piece of advice that I ever received in my life:

"Don't ever think that things will stay the same. Times were meant to change. Sometimes the changes are for the better, but often, changes are hard and for the worse." You can take that to the grave.

Now, food storage, sorry to say, is best handled by women because women are shoppers (the under-statement of the universe when it comes to American women). You know what food costs. You know what medical supplies, clothing, batteries and bottled water cost. What you don't know, however, is how to buy in large quantities or how to prepare for large quantities. There are many, many books and websites to teach you how to properly store food and water, and many websites that will help you know what to store in terms of medical supplies, medicines, etc.. But setting up a pantry is really the same as setting up a kitchen – just on a larger scale. And food storage, like gardening, is an art that develops over time. You get better at it year after year. Now, let's talk about what a rainy day is in the 21st Century:

Number one: Florida, Louisiana, Mississippi, and Alabama. Enough said.
Number two: Droughts and weather control technologies. Costs skyrocket during drought years.
Number three: Mt. St. Helens.
Number four: Terrorism of one sort or another. Today, tomorrow, but definitely again, and who knows where or how.
Number five: Believe it or not, the United States of America is flat broke and you probably are, too. Times are going to change and very soon.
Number six: Martial Law – a system that is up and ready to roll.

Now is not the time for women to be incompetent, and yet many American women have become so. When you don't or won't cook, clean, save, be the primary caretakers of your children, or even wash your car, you have become incompetent. I'm not being unkind. I'm being honest because I worry. I worry for all American people, but I know for a fact that if women are out of sorts, children are endangered and vulnerable, and I see endangered and vulnerable children in my daycare every day. Now is the time to wake up and lay selfishness aside. Families need intelligent women. No one needs a funny-colored woman with neon teeth, credit cards, and her interior decorator. Children need nurturing mothers who are competent caregivers and care enough to cook for them. Children must learn how to be prudent and responsible, and they simply can't if you are an irresponsible spend thrift, shallow, and vain. Families need intelligent women. And, with as much love as I can muster, I say to you, knock it off and get with the program. You think your living conditions are permanent. Don't be stupid. Times are changing and you must be ready with skills intact. If you remain incompetent, I guarantee you that your children will suffer first, last, and for the rest of their lives. You need to begin today.

How Will Our Garden Grow?

I've burned wood for years. My environmentally minded friends don't approve of this. It's true, I do make smoke, but I don't burn natural gas or oil. So what causes the greatest threat to the environment? I thought it was cars and industry, but I guess it was me burning wood in my stove. At least I admit my crime. But we love burning wood. It makes our house smell good and our house is warm, really warm. And we can toast marshmallows and make camp sandwiches and s'mores every day. We like the wood and the gathering. We like the whole process, though we do make smoke.

We also like to plant. This began with my grandfather and grandmother who loved flower gardens, and who grew food to eat in the late 1800's, early 1900's, and through the Great Depression. And my parents picked up the bug. My dad did yard maintenance and mom planted. She was mostly a flower gardener because she had been thoroughly used as a child to plant vegetables and to weed large food gardens during planting seasons. To be truthful, she never grew another vegetable garden after the mid 1950's. By that time, she hated the work, but luckily, I always liked the idea of growing food – another romanticism on my part—but to this day, I feel good when I'm tending soil and planting. Gardening has stayed miraculously fascinating to me, and I owe this love to beloved ancestors.

When I moved to my home eight years ago, I incorporated my daycare children into my gardening. If they could hold a packet of seed, they could plant. So, over the years, my youngest child, my daycare children, and I planted gardens – flowers, fruit, and vegetable. Year after year, we dug and planted. And we planted fun stuff, too! Giant sunflowers, pumpkins, little gourds, other squashes of all kinds, cherry tomatoes, melons, raspberries, and every animal-attracting flower we could find. And after we finally planted every square inch of the back yard, we tore it out and started over. And my children helped me. My 32-year-old daughter planted the bee, hummingbird, and monarch butterfly garden. My youngest daughter and granddaughters planted the zinnia beds, the sunflowers, and the squash and gourd beds. We've had fun doing this for many years. And it saddens me to no end that people do not plant anymore. But worse, it scares me to death that people think growing can be learned in one season or is simply not needed anymore. That, my women friends, is a fatal mistake and one that you do not want to pass on to your children. Let me explain.

I have been planting gardens since I can remember. I'm pretty good at it, but gardening, and especially food growing, is a combination of book learning, math, experimentation, a thousand mistakes, and a whole lot of intuition that, if ignored, brings fundamental failure to gardens. And most importantly, gardening is a family chore and duty.

As the most spoiled rotten people on the face of the earth, white, American women think that going to the grocery store is a pain, a chore, and a task that they can't escape. True enough...it's all those things, but we take for granted that everything we want and need at the store will be there tomorrow and the next day and next. We never consider that things we require won't be there. But consider this: After the East Coast black-out several years ago, every grocery store, every single one, was sold out of water, bread, peanut butter, and other non-perishables in less than two hours. Every single grocery store in the blackout areas – from New York to Ohio and into Canada. Every single battery was also sold out.

For better or worse, women "feel" responsible for feeding people. It's another old, primordial, biological yank that we deal with every day of our lives, and assuming that grocery stores will always be full of food is a dangerous path. Ask the people in post-hurricane Florida, Louisiana, Mississippi, and Alabama about their stores. Ask the people on both sides of the Mississippi River, during the floods of the 1990's about their grocery stores. Empty. And then consider drought, eco-fires, and our new and certain futures, which will bring attacks in one form or another back to American soil. My advice is to imagine the worst-case scenario, and then consider what it would take to safeguard your families for three to six months – or more.

Gardening is a soulful task and difficult for me to explain. It's a meditation, spirit calming, and gardening makes you feel better because it unclogs your brain. It opens something within so that the ability to silently think, pray, or reflect is available during daylight hours. I can't explain it well, but it has something to do with performing an ancient task of ancestry, touching the Earth itself, being in direct contact with its creatures, smelling the soil, feeling the air and sun – something opens from within and leaves us, in essence, quieted down in the mind and available for input. I've found that the reception, for lack of better words, is fulfilling, connecting, satisfying, and wonderfully, gently joyful. It's the same sense I have walking into large forests or swimming in lakes– it has something to do with our being in our place – not above or below anything – just simply in our place in the midst of life.

One of the greatest gifts you can give to your children is to teach them to garden and to grow food. Have them till, plant, weed, and water with you. You will be surprised how few words will be spoken, and yet the experiences will create life long memories. And don't do it once. Garden year after year so that you and your children learn the ways of nature and growing. We have clearly become too distanced from nature because we've forgotten that nature can have daily effects on our well being, but we have to participate in its genius.

Now days, people plant tomatoes in containers. Don't do that, and plant more than tomatoes. Plant spinach, squash, fruits, potatoes, onions, carrots, cucumbers and tomatoes. Learn how to grow food. And buy and store heirloom seeds so that you can collect pollinating seeds and replant next season. Beware of genetically altered seed. You cannot assume in today's world, just like yesterday's world (and last week's world), that food will always be readily available. I am as sure as rain that today's American women need to garden to begin the restoration of who they are and why they are important. I see sad and unhappy women everywhere, and I see their children who are soulfully suffering and not knowing why. This is one step to take that will reconnect women to their children and children to joy.

You have the Internet to get garden plans of any size and kind. Garden as a family. Once you start, you will never stop, and the healing of the soul will begin as you feed your minds and bodies with the mysteries of God's nature, growth, and perspective in a crazy world. If you take nothing from this book, please, just this—do this for your children. It will change the way you feel about yourselves, and your children will see you in another light – a real one.

Once you've grown food, you can discover canning, which is also good family fun that fuels knowledge, safety, cooking, prudence, and common sense.

A Last Look at Hearth and Home

We've verified through experience that men are, at best, peculiar helpers around the house. Children, by their very natures, are house cyclones. If they aren't, they are not acting like active and normal children. So, here we stand, the women of the house. Let's investigate this a bit further.

If the house is a wreck, if the dishes are not done, if there is hair on the bathroom floor, in the sink, in the shower drain, and on the counter; if the sweeper has not been run and there is dust on the book shelves; if there is pet food on the floor and fingerprints on the sliding glass door and near every light switch in the house; if the toilets are not sparkling and there are crumbs under the cushions and cob webs in the corners and cat fur on the couch, it is the woman who feels guilt. It is the woman who is embarrassed.

If the drive-thru bags are on the kitchen table, and the trash can is full, and the mail is spread out all over the counter, and a coffee cup ring is unwiped; if there are clothes on the floor and the laundry is not put away and the grass needs to be cut and the windows need to be washed, again – it is the woman who feels guilty. Why is this? Do not husbands and children greatly assist with the standard messes made in homes? Do they not leave wet towels unfolded and on the counter? Do they not use the dishes and the clothing? Indeed, they do, but they do not feel guilt over house messes. When your neighbors, friends, parents, and meter-reader make their unexpected arrivals, and the house is messy, do husband and children feel very uncomfortable because the house isn't perfect? No, in fact, not at all. We, the women, feel guilty and very, very uncomfortable. Why?

Here's my proposal: I propose that we are primordially connected to "houses." I believe that "the home" has been the domain of females since the beginning of time, as we had to be responsible for creating safe and warm havens for babies. I propose that the female gender is connected to the home through biology beginning with the first childbearing woman on the planet.

We are not outdoor creatures. Humans are required by necessity to be sheltered solidly from the elements. And I believe that throughout human history, women created homes based upon the needs of children and, particularly, infants. The house is our instinctual domain because, first and foremost, it is our primordial nest. In this way, we differ not from the rest of God's female creatures. We are nest builders by virtue of survival. The house is ours, and we intuitively sense its importance. The house is ours and most women feel this way. The men may live there and even pay for it, but the house is absolutely and unequivocally ours from an instinctual and emotional point of necessity.

The lack of cooking and concern for the nutrition of children, coupled with the bizarre rituals of today's female concerning her house, tell me, without fail, that American women are functioning less and less as biological females. However, they still intuit themselves as the outright head of the house. And I'd venture to say that this ancient instinct, that of nest builder, is exactly why servants never suit us. House cleaners and crews don't do a good enough job. They can't sense what we think obviously needs to be done. Truthfully, they can't because we have instinctual priorities when it comes to house keeping. Every woman has unique and sometimes odd priorities that matter significantly in regards to how she wants her house cleaned, straightened, and prepared. This is why husbands can never do house chores they way we want them done. This is why children never satisfy us after cleaning their rooms, and why maids never get it right. The house is our biological domain. We have a fundamental, internal clarity of how our homes need to be, and it is different for every woman.

The house remains ours, but we are clearly pulling away, as mothers, from the nest. The result is obvious. The nest is becoming far less comfortable and more professional in ambience. It is becoming less welcoming and unnatural, and the primary reason is because women, who biologically create and produce comforts for children, are not creating home comforts like foods and the traditional arts and crafts of mothers – all of which having historically developed for "the family." The home is becoming sterilized and an ineffective place for people to grow, learn, and feel safe and sheltered. It is becoming more a gallery of social status than a home.

This will have dire consequences for children who emotionally attach themselves to homes and their memories of them. The events of their childhoods dictate their learning patterns for parenthood. Their homes create senses of security and talents that they will take into adulthood. Without them, the family will grow in more clinical terms and will be far less important to them than entertainments and careers. And this leaves your future grandchildren at risk of even far greater sterilizations of family culture, traditions, and concepts.

The happy childhood is clearly changing. We don't yet know what this will mean in 50 years, but again I say – the altering of the most fundamental relationship – that of mother and child—is dangerous, if not anti-biology. And it's frightening to even consider what that could really mean. Also note that many, many politically funded "think tanks" have declared the need and intention to dismantle the traditional American family.

And finally, if you stupidly got caught in the lenders' low interest rate scams and purchased a large, expensive home that you know costs too much to keep and maintain, get rid of it NOW. The value of homes is going to fall very, very soon. All economists are now predicting that homes may loose about 25 to 40 % of their value when the housing bubble bursts. This is no joke. Sell the monument to your pretend social status and buy a sensible house that you can afford. Millions and millions of Americans have put themselves in jeopardy via the low interest rate manipulation, which was the only way to uphold the American economy and fight off recession as our government bankrupted itself with wars, national security, and "terrorism." Get yourselves out of debt NOW. Don't think things are not going to change. It's happening as we speak and as quietly and quickly as possible. Millions of people are going to lose their homes, and particularly the ones who have taken out variable rate equity loans. The cheap money that was made available to us over the last five years for automobiles and houses was in effort to maintain our economy by getting you to borrow and spend – all with the intention of taking your private property. You need to understand this and you must, must believe it. Wages have not risen in the United States for nearly 20 years, and yet, during this same period, middle class Americans bought huge houses because, via low interest rates, they could just, and I mean barely afford the payments. Lenders have started to raise interest rates, but they've only just begun. Rates will continue to rise for the next decade or maybe two. When the value of your giant house falls 30%, and your payments double, ask yourself how your monstrosity feels and looks now. Many of you are going to lose your giant houses, and your impending bankruptcies are not going to allow you to buy another – if you can even file for bankruptcy. Those laws have also been severely curtailed. Get rid of your MacMansion immediately. You cannot risk losing the roofs over the heads of your children. Scale down and live within sensible means. When you see sprawling, tens of thousands of new communities in every state in the U.S., with $200-$500,000.00 homes filled with parents raising little kids, you have to know that this is not reasonable. Young couples don't have this kind of money. And, according to the 2003 U.S. Census Income Report, the average wage for American families in 2003 was $43,527.00 per year. To see these communities, one would believe that the average American is making well over $100-200,000.00 per year, and that is simply not the case. Most Americans families live on $43,000.00 per year. Therefore, you know the middle class is in insane debt. You are not wealthy people, and you know it, and your giant houses are going to destroy you. Sell them while you can. Be proud of who you are. Don't let envy, greed, and lies define you.

My sisters in America, I have given you my best advice. I offer it based on my experiences with your beautiful children. There is no other agenda. If I have an agenda, it would be that I believe all children in America should be homeschooled, but that is another book being composed in my mind as we speak.

What Is a Wholesome Life in America?

A friend says I need to offer more answers to all the problems presented in this book. I think you need to find a genius for that order, but I'll make a simplistic stab at an alternative life style that may help to get women off the current crash course of ineptitude.

The first thing that comes to mind is that we should try to live wholesome lives, but, as with most things, wholesomeness is in the eyes of beholders, and especially so in America. Wholesomeness is difficult, because we are polluted by television and media. Our minds and souls are full of images and experiences that have permanently changed and left us without innocence. Therefore, wholesomeness must be chosen and fought for on an internal level. It is very, very difficult to live without the daily bombardment of cultural corruptions. And it is equally hard not to succumb to the numbness that results from these corruptions. If we accept corruption as normal, then all sense of good and bad, right and wrong becomes a gray area and, literally, anything goes. You have children to raise, so think this through carefully. To try to live a wholesome life, you have to work hard and you have to be steadfast and creative. Again, governmentally imposed cultural corruption is operating everywhere – and especially in the public school system.

There has always been a part of me that wanted to rid my house of all television sets. We know we are all addicted to television and that addiction is certainly counted on by big business. If we didn't watch television, what would we do? If we didn't use television sets to entertain our children and select our politicians, what would our kids do, and how would we know for whom to vote?

I think we would read and write a lot more. People from all cultures find and create entertainments. It seems to be a human need. Therefore, whether you discard your TVs or not, perhaps libraries and/or comfy reading rooms should be considered as requirements for good homes. Reading breeds thinking, soul searching, and critical analysis. Reading also breeds writing, which, in turn, breeds creative focus and critical self-evaluation. So let's begin with home libraries to at least curb the television habit.

Next, make the work of homes the responsibility of those who live in them. In other words, create your homes. Don't buy the creations of decorators and have them delivered into your lives. Do the work and the creative development yourselves, and let your children be involved in the processes and decisions that create their comforts. Teach yourselves to work together as families. Your homes will then mean something to you and your work will have value for everyone in the family. Develop real skills.

Grow food and flowers for your families. It is one of the most important skills that any person on the planet can have and the skill is at the core of our survival as a species. Growing food teaches you more than you will ever imagine. It awakens the oldest, primordial knowledge what you carry, and you will become more spiritual, more intelligent, and you will gain much-needed perspective about your importance and place as a living being on the planet. Growing food is more important than you can possibly imagine, but you will understand its importance the minute you harvest and prepare to plant again. Always buy heirloom seed. All other is genetically modified.

Equally, the understanding and participating in the stewardship of the natural world is the responsibility of all people and families. Modern consumerism and, in many ways, religion, has deadened our hearts to nature. We have become emotionally separate from it and we cannot do this and remain healthy. It is imperative that we reconnect ourselves to the fact that we are solely reliant upon nature and it's ecosystems. We are, physiologically, participating members of all Earth's ecosystems. And human brain development mandates that we all stay involved, on a daily basis, with the care and protection of all natural resources. Now, mind you, there is a HUGE difference between "conservation" and "sustainability." Conservation of Earth's natural resources is a moral obligation of all people on the planet. "Sustainability" is the land theft manipulation used to eliminate all private ownership of property. Local 21, Smart Growth, Sustainable Future, and all "visions" for the future are land theft language. Be very aware of this mass manipulation, and make sure you read the United Nations document called Agenda 21. "Sustainable nature" and "ecology" has now become the domain and global mandate of the United Nations and its land trust real estate thieves. "Sustainable" anything is global governance knocking at your local doors.

The mass use of pesticides and fertilizers for the past 40 years in suburban communities has had far-reaching and destructive results to insects, birds, pets, and to water. We have to stop putting poisons on the ground and call it yard maintenance. Read up on studies being conducted, as we speak, of the diseases and disappearance trends of common birds, insects, and amphibians. And also, study your community's water reports. Don't throw them away when you receive them in the mail. Nearly all fresh water in America is poor due to chemical contaminations. In fact, most Americans should have reverse-osmosis water filtration systems installed in their homes due to contaminated water. We have to change. We have polluted epidemically and caused mass deterioration and damage to subterranean and water life. And by doing so, we've risked the lives and futures of our children and grand children. We have got to take stewardship seriously from now on, and the only way to accomplish this is to realize, once and for all, that we are creatures, too. If the smaller creatures are sick and dying, so are we. Equally, the best stewards have always been property owners. Fight for your property rights, for they are being systematically taken – very systematically. Also, beware the current eco-governmental partnerships and land trust organizations. They are running on high speed with the intention of taking away your private property rights. If you lose these rights, you won't be growing food. Just ask a farmer, or better yet, just look at the sheer numbers of deed-restricted communities in every state in the nation. These "communities" are "Communitarian" communities. That means communities where you have no land and virtually no civil rights. Take great heed!

Also, the education of children begins and should end in the home. Public schools exist to create "regional" work forces for "regional" corporations. That is their function. However, they also create life styles and personality types and classism. The negative impact of twelve years of public education upon a child cannot be over emphasized or overstated. Adult occupations are determined, daily structures are determined, socio-economic groups are determined, social behaviors are determined, sexual identities are determined, sexual behaviors are determined, racial-social barriers are created, prejudices are created, world vision is created, and records about your children are kept by the government as public schools are solely global-governmental institutions. Is this how and where you want your child educated? We've been told for at least the last 30 years that American children's educations are deplorable. I agree. And I also believe that education is in the eye of the beholder or should be. If you must send your children to public schools, you will have to hope for the best. Your child will graduate with a low to mediocre utilitarian education. If that's good enough for your child, then so be it. If you want your child to be educated with creativity and fascinations, and a whole world of curricula, then you're going to have to do it yourself. I repeat, if you want your children to have truly extraordinary educations, you are going to have to do it yourselves. And your child doesn't need eight hours of instruction a day to become brilliant. I've heard that teachers actually teach about three to four hours a day in schools. That should tell you something right there about the spending of your tax dollars by the government. Home schooling also removes the insidious school bus culture, the horrible lunch room food, the inability to choose good teachers for your kids, and the plain and simple truth that many, many children are afraid to go to schools due to their mistreatment by bullies, thugs, bad teachers, and the horrible influences of kiddy campus cultures and their paid government and Socialist employees. Public education needs to be critically analyzed by parents for what it is and is not. Never assume that public schools provide good educations. They do not. They provide paid indoctrination specialists who thrive off your tax dollars while eliminating your rights as parents.

Next, think about materialism. I know it is a buzzword of the hippy culture, but so what? In spite of the trashing of the 1960's and 1970's, there were enlightenments that came out of that time, as well. If we live with fewer entertainments, we operate differently and more creatively. We focus more upon people than things, and we live uncluttered lives. I cannot reiterate enough that by getting rid of your clutter, all the things you have and do not use, will create easier environments in homes. Clutter and stuff becomes something else to be responsible for, and it causes anxiety. As you get older, you realize even more the anxiety that all your stuff imposes upon you. Get rid of things you don't have a use for. And don't buy every new technology that comes down the pike. You do not need to buy new and upgraded cell phones every two years – especially since there are now (il)legally bugged.

Also, make every attempt to earn income from your homes. The two working parents routine is too difficult. Children need parents who are home when they are home. I realize our employment culture is not set up this way, but as good parents, we have to put our children and their safety, stability, and happiness over and above jobs. It can be done. Yes, it can.

Please, rid yourselves of the pressures of American beauty. If you spend more than 20 minutes on your hair, cut it or let it grow long and wear braids.

Wear make-up for special occasions and forget about it for everyday living. The tanning, nail parlors, teeth bleaching, manicures, pedicures, massages, and plastic surgeries – just stop it. It's a waste of money, a waste of time, and it breed self-absorption and self-loathing. In other words, it's vanity, which is meaningless and damaging to the intellect and to the spirit.

Together as families, prepare for rainy days. Store some food and supplies, medicines and water, and use the wisdoms of the past to ensure your future. Save money. Drive sensible cars. Rein yourselves in so that you can achieve comfort in your families. Debt destroys comfort and marriages.

There are, of course, a thousand other things we can do to change the course of gender definition, but purpose is the true root of change. Family businesses are something to consider, but something with purpose that gives internal value to the people in families and to the real natural world and animals would be my best guess. As I've said, women need to define themselves so that they don't fall victim to the definitions of others. Self-determination and definition is the key to real freedom. Politically defined "feminism" is abject enslavement.

Defining Yourself Begins With an Erased Slate

Nearing the end of this book, I wish I had more answers. They are so difficult to find for, in the great scheme of time, the changes that have brought women to this place in history are terribly new. History says one thing about who and what we have been, while contemporary sociologists, marketing entities, business, and feminists now say something else. So my first inclination – my first best guess is this: Let's stop listening to everyone and think about who we are, what we are, and what we want to be. We have earned the right to self-definition and self-determination. It seems that the second women were free, business entities, entertainment entities, and political and religious groups with agendas immediately stepped into history's place and redefined our new freedoms, purposes, places, and our new and improved looks. I'm tired of being told how I should be. How about you?

As free women, it's time to develop and define our roles, and especially, and from now on, to define beauty to ourselves, for ourselves. We need to take created and manipulated female aesthetics out of the hands of media and marketing and determine, for ourselves, how we want to look, for the perfect woman is not a woman at all – she is a photograph. Our competition with her forces us to lose, and our only hope for real peace and acceptance of ourselves is to throw away her glossy emptiness.

If American women continue to be defined by media and big business, then we have already thrown away true freedom. We are disrespecting women throughout all history and, particularly, those who are still living lives that are controlled and defined by others.

Now, in the 21st Century, many of us have taken our freedoms and used them for shallow and purposeless desires. We have become pathologically materialistic, pathologically vain and self-absorbed, and we have lost all the innate skills that saved us throughout human history. Now, we deserve rather than earn. We demand rather than create. We expect rather than put forth time and effort. We play shallow games and spend shallow time rather than giving of ourselves to greater purposes. This is embarrassing on a worldwide scale and it simply has to stop because it's warping our children.

Next, we must define for ourselves, and away from the influences of political agendas, who and what it is we want to be. We must begin with a blank slate. Do we want to be males? Do we want to be rich, young models in mansions? Do we want to be mothers and wives? Do we want money more than anything else? To all of these things, I say no – not really. So the true and honest question is, what do the free women of American want to be? And are they willing to do the emotional and physical self-investigations to find out? Take away the historical and cultural definitions of contemporary, American women, and who are we? Living in debt in McMansion communities? Pretending to be wealthy? Pretending to be richly and exceptionally beautiful? Pretending to be the social elite? Pretending to be better than others? And above all else, pretending to be happy and contented? I think today's women are too often angry and miserable. It's way past time to take charge of our unhappiness and miseries and to quit blaming them on others. After all, we are free to do as we please.

And I hope and pray for families. Marriage, and the traditional roles of mothers and fathers raising children, is unwell in the United States. It's unwell as a human foundation, and it is getting sicker every year in our country. We can have all the elections and political groups and pressures the country can muster, but I believe that the survival of marriage is actually in the hands of women. We have the children and we file most of the divorces papers. Personally, I hope the institution of marriage can survive. It's one of the oldest traditions of human beings. If it doesn't survive, I expect the changes for humans will be far-reaching and long-term. Would it be better if marriage changed or was eliminated? We don't know. There is no precedent. We could ask the half of American children who have had marriages fail in their families for advice. We could talk to single parents about raising children by themselves. We could talk to unmarried couples raising children for input, but ultimately, I believe the future of marriage rests in the hand of contemporary and future women. As marriage surely began as the protection and feeding of women and their infants, maybe times have changed enough that women have so little need of males that marriage is simply retrograde in modern culture.

I personally hope marriage can survive. It's the romantic in me, I guess, and it has a lot to do with my respect for the nature of biology and its two unique sides. I believe that women have awesome responsibilities in the world. This is one of them, and it will certainly be interesting to see what women decide to do.

And finally, I pray that American women can find greater purpose and use for their gender. We have really lessened ourselves in the last 40 years, and it is terribly visible in our communities and schools, on television, and within medical communities. It's visible in the sheer numbers of stores, beauty parlors, spas, tanning and nail salons, the exercise and workout industries, the shopping channels, and in the overly decorated American homes. We simply have to stop, look, consider, and think about what we, as a gender, have created and support. This is the best we can do with our precious freedom?

I hoped for art and brilliance. I hoped for all that pent-up brainpower to aid the world with genius and nurturing and compassion, and with answers that were born from the tremendous survival skills and wisdoms of women. I hoped for old, intuitive instincts and thoughts to further civilize and ease the world of men, war, and power lust. But it's not there and it's not happening. So I end this book with a request – just a request, which is this: Can we please think it over? Can we consider the thoughts of one ordinary person, who is your neighbor, who lives around the corner from you? Will you hear me this one time? I'm no expert so you can take or leave all of this, but will you please just think it through? It's time for women to reflect, evolve, and find true purpose in freedom. And remember, self-definition doesn't begin with political or corporate agendas. Remember that next time you look at a model in a magazine.

Finally, dear American women, return to faith. Read the Bible, which is a process – a lifelong process. You're not expected to master its meaning in one reading. Meaning evolves with maturity and experience, children and grandchildren, marriage and tragedy, happiness and loss, and daily living. Someone once told me to put Biblical questions on my "spiritual shelf." In other words, don't expect to understand everything all at once. If there is something you don't understand, or something you disagree with, put those issues on your spiritual shelf, and come back to them later in your life. God understands how difficult faith can be in a corrupting culture and world. God is patient. You be patient with faith, too. It grows and evolves in mysterious ways.

The Intuition Checklist

How do you know if your intuition has declined? How do you know if you're not operating on all female cylinders? Try the checklist:

Do frequently feel annoyed and overburdened?
Are you awake nights and exhausted during the days?
Do messes in your house frequently infuriate you?
Are you and your husband frequently at silent odds?
Are you often annoyed or angry with your children?
Are macaroni and cheese, pizza, and one or two item meals typical of dinners in your home?
Are your refrigerators frequently rather empty?
Do you spend an hour or more, daily, on hair, make-up, and wardrobe, and will you leave the house without make-up?
Have you opted for liposuction, implants, or plastic surgery? And do you want more?
Do you find that your children really don't give you much joy?
Do your husband and children frequently embarrass you?
Are you quick to criticize them, and are you sarcastic toward them?
Do you feel superior to and more intelligent than your husband?
Are you obsessed with your face, weight, and figure?
Have you joined a gym? Bleached your teeth? Opted for false nails?
Have you taken vacations you cannot afford?
Do you own more than four or five pairs of shoes?
Is your house loaded with decorations and knick-knacks?
Can you not afford to buy couches and chairs?
Do you have any money in a savings account, mutual fund, or IRA? Do you own any gold or silver?
Are you happiest when you are alone or shopping?

Do you have anything, at all, put back for emergencies – money, food, water, medical supplies, batteries, toilet paper, soaps, diapers, baby formula, pet foods, etc.?
Do you wait until the last second to get your children up in the morning before you take them to daycare?
Do maids and laborers frequently not satisfy you?
Do your children watch television constantly and do they get upset if you turn off the television? Are they chronic video gamers?
Are you cash poor? Do your monthly bills take all your cash?
Do you drink alcohol, take supplements, and diet every day?
Do landscaping contractors put in your gardens and beds?
Can you take criticism from your children, parents, or husband without anger and defensiveness?

You get the gist. If you are operating in the best interest of the health and happiness of your families, then the answers to these questions are obvious. If the answers are not obvious to you, or if you are now angry because of this list or book, then you need a lot of self-examination about the life you live and your role as a female. Consider the memories that you are creating, both as a parent and of the childhood home. Consider how long the man in your house can continue to be engaged by your spending, anger, and incompetence. Always remember that men are far more dependent on women than women have ever been on men. They need you to be intelligent and competent managing the nest, and don't ever waste hard earned money.

It is surely time to end this book for I have said all that I can. I am grateful to all who took the time to read my words and hear my concerns. I am grateful, and only hope that something made sense. We are so strong and have come such a long distance in history. To now become angry dolls, resenting what we should treasure, and lose our strengths as women, would be the greatest of indignities to our ancestors who struggled for life and prayed for the freedoms we ignore. Always remember that we have come from enslavements to luxuries, and that most women on the planet still live, in one way or another, as enslaved human beings. The worst way to take this for granted is to believe that you, as one person, deserve more than any other. Be humble. Be grateful for your lives and your families, and make your homes and deeds demonstrate civility and the genius of womanhood. Don't live envious, greedy lies and warp the identities and futures of your children. Make your children proud of your character. Demonstrate love in deeds.

Create homes based on your love for the people inside them. Make them warm and comfortable and a reflection of your effort. And last, but not least, care for your children. They are not your possessions or your interruptions but blessings given to you to guard, to teach, and love. They are your only legacies, and they will ultimately judge your parenting—and you will be judged by all others based upon the condition of your children as adults.

Finally, prepare for unexpected changes by staying alert and courting wisdom. Use your intuition. When "things" feel off, or uncomfortable, or you sense the need to do something—listen and act. These sensations are one of the greatest gifts you have been given as a female. If you feel and know you are financially overextended, act. If you are concerned about the behaviors of your children, act. Change your behaviors to make conditions better and kinder for your families. Don't wait. And never mistake mean-spiritedness for feminism. We are here to pass tests. Don't fail them, and by doing so fail all you love, including your country and your beliefs. May God continue to bless our lives, our Constitution, and our sovereign nation, which gave freedom to American women. Be dutiful and loyal to families and nation.

Endnotes

I'd like to thank my mother, daughters, and grandchildren for their love and life-long inspirations. Equally, I'd like to thank my Sister who has been a living example of a brilliant parent, wife, cook, gardener, housewife, and professional, working woman.

I'd like to thank my dear friend, Molly, who has been a blessing of a friend for two decades, and my dear friend Jennifer who has helped me in a thousand ways to be smarter, wiser, more spiritually aware, sensitive, and confident.

I'd like to thank my Father, a kind, gentle, and skilled man who loved and enjoyed his family, and who was loved and greatly needed in return.

I'd like to thank master investor Jim Rogers who gave me some of the best advice I ever received in my life. He said, "Always invest in what you know." He, with my daycare children, inspired the writing of this book. Thank you, Mr. Rogers. You were right.

And to my beloved daycare children, I simply love each and every one of you and will never forget you. May your lives be joyful, and may you grow to be free people – God willing.